SALOME, from the painting by A. G. H. Regnault

The Princess Salome—the daughter of Herodias.

UNDER
PONTIUS PILATE

Being a part of the correspondence between

Caius Claudius Proculus in Judea

and

Lucius Domitius Ahenobarbus at Athens

In the years 28 and 29 A.D.

TRANSLATED AND EDITED BY
WILLIAM SCHUYLER

Fredonia Books
Amsterdam, The Netherlands

Under Pontius Pilate

Translated and Edited by
William Schuyler

ISBN: 1-4101-0765-5

Reprinted from the 1906 edition

Fredonia Books
Amsterdam, The Netherlands
http://www.fredoniabooks.com

CONTENTS

PART I

THE SON OF MAN

Contents

PART II

THE SON OF GOD

LIST OF ILLUSTRATIONS

TRANSLATOR'S NOTE

In his attempt to turn into English the following letters of Caius Claudius Proculus and his friend, which are as full of Latin colloquialisms as the famous correspondence of the great Cicero, the translator has not only found it necessary to render the Latin *tu* by *you*, but also to avail himself of numerous English colloquialisms of the present day in order to preserve as much as possible the easy-going, modern spirit of the original. For the educated Romans of the first century of our era were in many ways as "modern" as, if not more modern than, the Americans of the twentieth. Likewise, as the sayings of the Nazarene that are given by Caius Claudius are quoted from memory in Latin, and naturally differ in some unimportant points from the Greek texts of the Gospels, the translator has thought it best for the sake of unity to turn them from the Latin into modern

TRANSLATOR'S NOTE

English rather than to quote the corresponding passages from the beautiful tho antiquated "Authorized Version" of the English Bible.

As to the paraphrases of the Latin verses with which Caius Claudius adorned several of his letters, the translator must acknowledge his indebtedness to A. S. M. Chisholm, M.D., of Bennington, Vermont.

" . . . For the right faith is, that we believe and confess; that our Lord Jesus Christ, the Son of God, is God and Man;

God, of the Substance of the Father, begotten before the worlds; and Man, of the Substance of his Mother, born in the world;

Perfect God, and perfect Man, of a reasonable soul and human flesh subsisting;

Equal to the Father, as touching his Godhead; and inferior to the Father, as touching his manhood.

Who altho he be God and Man, yet he is not two, but one Christ;

One; not by conversion of the Godhead into flesh, but by the taking of the Manhood into God;

One altogether; not by confusion of substance, but by Unity of Person.

For as the reasonable soul and flesh is one man; so is God and Man one Christ."

From the Athanasian Creed.

Part I

THE SON OF MAN

I

The Procurator

I

Caius Claudius Proculus in Cæsarea of Judea to Lucius Domitius Ahenobarbus in Athens, sends greeting.

S. V., B. E., E. V.* Your letter, found here on my return from Jerusalem, filled me with delight; because you, my Lucius,—the contemplator, the philosopher, the Stoic,—desire to be kept informed of the acts of Proculus,—the worldling, the pleasure-seeker, in short the Epicurean. I suppose that you, in the quiet shades of your philosophic retreat, have occasional longings for the blinding glare of the Syrian sun; just as I, in the midst of this fierce life, think sometimes with pleasure of your nebulous dreams. Be that as it may, you know that I love you as fervently now as I did when we first began our studies at

* *Si valeas, bene est; ego valeo.* "If you are in good health, it is well; I too am in good health."

3

UNDER PONTIUS PILATE

Athens with Sosius, and consequently your slightest request is my law. Therefore I here begin these *Commentarii de Vita C. Claudii Proculi in Judæa.* They may not be as important as the commentaries of the divine Julius Cæsar, or as interesting as the letters of the famous Cicero, or as perfect as the epistles in verse of the delightful Horatius Flaccus; but I know that they will be as truthful as the first, as frank as the second, and far more careless than the last.

I hope in return to receive from you some subtle stoical disquisitions as a relief from the prevailing thoughtlessness here. For in the ceaseless round of military duties, public shows, and jovial feasts, a man who has once learned to think likes occasionally to be reminded that he has a mind. And I am sure that out of pity, if for no other reason, you will grant my request.

As I told you in Athens, life is vivid here in Judea. These Jews with their strange superstitions are the most energetic people in the world. This great city of Cæsarea, with its spacious harbor and its magnificent breakwater two hundred feet broad, was built in a few years by the great

THE PROCURATOR

Herod as a testimonial to the divine Augustus Cæsar. You may remember something of Herod the Great, that strange Jewish king who died some thirty years ago. He managed to keep on the best of terms with the divine Julius, with Marcus Antonius, and with the divine Augustus; he made wide conquests, and erected magnificent buildings like the Antonia Tower and the great Temple in Jerusalem; and then, from fear of growing idle, slaughtered his subjects, and even his wives and children, whenever he needed a little extra excitement. But so great is the fecundity of these Jews, that when Herod finally passed away, he still left some subjects to be ruled and some children to rule over them.

When I came here with my uncle Pontius Pilate a couple of years ago, the first thing we discovered was that this Jewish intensity had diminished not one whit since Herod's death. You see, the procurator, altho his headquarters are at Cæsarea, must be in Jerusalem through all the high festivals. Now these Jews have some half dozen great festivals every year, and they allow their pugnacious as well as their religious natures full swing while they are under the special influence of their mysterious god. They are divided into two great sects, Pharisees and Sadducees (somewhat like our Stoics and Epicureans), and besides are separated by locality into Judeans, Pereans, Galileans, Samaritans, and so on. All of these separate groups hate each other with the same intensity with which they adore their common and only god, and the slaughter of men in the streets as well as of beasts in the Temple is the usual method of celebrating their feasts. So you see, a procurator can not afford to be absent from the capital at such lively times, as Coponius found out to his cost in the days of Judas the Gaulonite some score of years ago.

Therefore my good uncle, the procurator, with rare military foresight, and because he hates long journeys, decided to have his headquarters in Jerusalem, and sent up a detachment with the standards to make things ready for the grand entrance of Cæsar's representative. He knew a little of the character of the people—tho not much —and occupied the Antonia Tower by night with a cohort which displayed the Roman standards

early the next morning. Of course he expected
a mob, because these silly Jews allow no images
whatsoever in their sacred city—that was why
he waited in Cæsarea; but he was utterly un-
prepared for what did happen. The mob of
Jerusalem assembled as usual, but they left the
innocent soldiers alone and trooped all the way
to Cæsarea, some seventy miles or so.

Here they practically besieged the procurator
in his palace—bombarding him, not with stones
or javelins, but with weeping and howling, with
prayers and imprecations—which I assure you
was very much worse,—while every now and then
there would be a special attack made by some
learned Jew who would talk and argue till he made
your head swim. Finally, on the fifth day my
uncle Pontius lost patience, had the mob surrounded by a few centuries of legionaries, and
announced from his balcony that if they did not
raise the siege he would have them all slain.
With a howl they bared their necks and declared
that they were ready to die any kind of death
rather than live to see the "holy city" profaned
by images of heathen gods. Here was a pretty

situation for a man just entering on a procurator-ship! And to make matters worse my good aunt Claudia interfered in their favor. You may imagine my surprise.

To conclude this long story, the good Pontius, who is not any too strong in spirit, yielded, recalled the troops and standards, and the mob flowed back to Jerusalem extolling him and the Emperor. But down in the bottom of their Jewish hearts I know they thought him weak enough. They are like those patients who do not think the physician does his duty by them unless he bleeds them frequently and copiously.

Herod understood them perfectly, and the good Pontius had to come to his method of managing the Jews after all. For when he wanted to build a much needed aqueduct at Jerusalem and tried to use some of their "Corban," or Temple tribute —which they squander in all sorts of inanities— they got so abominably rebellious and riotous at this "desecration of the sacred shekels" that he had to surround them with a lot of soldiers in common clothes and with concealed daggers. After a few thousand or so of them had their throats

8

cut, they were silenced and admitted Pilate's authority. You see the mistake of all tender-hearted men. Had he not yielded to the mob in Cæsarea he never would have had this trouble in Jerusalem. You remember how the divine Julius "pacified all Gaul." Well, there was a man who knew how to handle barbarians!

Moreover, because Pilate did not send his legionaries out in full armor with their ensigns and standards, he had to do the business all over again. For at the last festival I attended—I have forgotten the name of it—a mob of Galileans got into the Temple court and held it against all comers, letting nobody else sacrifice. The uproar finally became unbearable and a century of legionaries had to silence the disturbance by mixing the blood of the pugnacious Galileans with their sacrifices. Affairs have been somewhat quieter since then, as Caiaphas, the high priest, and Annas, his father-in-law, are strong supporters of Cæsar's power. I don't think they care a denarius for their religion, but their revenues are something magnificent.

Speaking of that last festival, my chief amuse-

ment in Jerusalem has lately been furnished by
a fascinating bit of Oriental beauty. Mary of
Magdala is her name—a woman of really excellent Jewish family, and even of considerable
wealth. As for beauty, I have never seen her
equal. Her combination of rose-red lips, red-
brown eyes, and red-gold hair is irresistible.
The Jews say she has seven devils, but I know
personally that she has at least seventy. If I
could have prevailed upon her I should have
brought her here to this Roman town where her
delightful devils would have a fair chance. But
Mary, after all, is a Jewess, and even she considered sometimes that she had gòne too far by
admitting me, a Gentile, into her intimacy. I
happen to know that this particular thing has been
brought forward by the good Pharisees as absolute evidence of her devils. However, whether
it was of herself or of her devils—who might have
come from Rome—I know not; but certainly I
have never been better entertained in my life—
the Greek girls *know*, but these Orientals *are*.

So, when I went to Jerusalem for that last feast,
I looked out for her the first thing, but found that

she had gone with quite a train of hangers-on to
an estate of hers near Magdala, on the Sea of
Galilee, in the domain of the tetrarch Herod Antipas, son of old Herod the Great. I had my freedman, Syrus, hunt up her brother Lazarus, who
has considerable property in Jerusalem, but
Lazarus did not want even her name mentioned—
on account of her devils and Romans, I suppose,
as he is a prominent Pharisee. Then Syrus
investigated on his own account, and finally discovered the reason of Mary's sudden departure.

There is a new prophet, *rabbi*, or "master,"
arisen in Galilee—somewhat like a certain John
who preached and baptized near the Dead Sea
last year, only this man is not so fierce as he and
draws even bigger crowds by his eloquence—
these Jews being as fond of religious exhortation
as we Romans are of forensic oratory. This new
"master" came up at one of the feasts to Jerusalem, where Mary saw him and was fascinated.
According to Syrus, some of the Galileans think
he is the promised King of Israel, or "Messiah"
as they call him, who is to free the Jews and make
them masters of the whole earth; others say that

he is only a carpenter of Nazareth, named Joshua
—or Jesus, as the Greeks write it—and that he is
too lazy to work and so goes about living off other
people and occasionally performing miracles.
Syrus told me some wonderful tales of these same
miracles—such as making the lame to walk, the
blind to see, in short, the same things as are
related of Apollonius at Tyana, and of some other
wizards in this marvelous Orient. But:

"I cannot, like Apella, the Jew, believe it.
  The tranquil gods,—'tis from wise men of old we receive it—
  Repose in careless ease in the heavens yonder,
  And lazily scorn the tribute of human wonder." *

Yet, whatever this man may be in reality, the
performance of Mary is in full keeping with her
character—always looking for some new sensation.
After having subdued a Roman noble, she evidently is not to be satisfied with anything else for
a triumph than a prophet or perhaps a heaven-
sent king.

When I returned to Cæsarea, I told my uncle

* . . . Credat Judæus Apella
  Non ego; namque deos didici securum agere ævum
  Nec, si quid miri faciat natura, deos id
  Tristes exalto cœli demittere tecto.—*Horace*.

Pilate all I knew about this new prophet, which quite alarmed him, as he is always fearing another Gaulonitish Judas. My aunt Claudia, however, was much interested. Do you know, I believe she is already almost a Jewish proselyte! Nearly all of her servants and slaves are Israelites, and they read to her constantly from their sacred books. So she had a lot of questions to ask me about this Jesus—more, in fact, than I could answer.

During our conversation a brilliant idea occurred to me. I proposed to my uncle that he should send me on a mission to Herod in Galilee, and I promised that while I was there I would find out how much danger there was to be expected from this new prophet. Pilate agreed immediately with the proposal, especially as it would give him an opportunity of conciliating Herod Antipas, with whom he has been somewhat at outs since that slaughter of the Galileans in the Temple. As you have probably divined, the prospect of meeting again with the fair Mary of Magdala and her numerous devils was what prompted my urging this little mission.

UNDER PONTIUS PILATE

I start in a day or two with a small retinue, and shall write you further of my success; if not on the way, then on my return. Take care of your health, my Lucius. Farewell.

II

The Disciples

II

At Tiberias

HERE I am, my Lucius, in this new-fledged city
built by Herod Antipas and named in honor of
the divine Tiberius Cæsar. It is another Cæsarea
—on a smaller scale, of course,—and has a beautiful
situation on the shore between the hills and the
lake. The town is filled with Greeks, Romans,
Syrians, Phœnicians. In fact, almost every race
is to be found here in considerable numbers, ex-
cepting, however, the Jews, most of whom keep
out of the city, not only because it is built on the
site of an old cemetery, but because of the temples
and the statues of the gods which act on them like
a red cloak on a mad bull. How strange it is
that rational beings can be so absurd as to be
disturbed by beautiful images of what they well
know are utterly imaginary personages even if a
few ignoramuses do bow down and worship them!

UNDER PONTIUS PILATE

I shall have to stay here for a week or so, till the messenger I shall send to Pilate returns with his answer. It is by him that I send this letter. You must know that when I arrived here, I found that Herod had left some time ago in order to carry on war against Aretas, the king of Arabia Petra. It is the old story—as old as Helen of Troy—and the "most foul cause of war"* this time is the beautiful Herodias, formerly the wife of Herod's half-brother Philip. I saw her in Rome with Antipas just before I left for Cæsarea, and, tho she will never see thirty again, she can turn any man's head for years to come. I heard that she promised to divorce her stupid husband for the fiery Antipas, if he on his part would get rid of his own encumbrance. The infatuated Herod agreed to this, and the intense pair cemented their union before they left home for Galilee. Philip made not the least objection to the transaction, as perhaps he is not tuned up to the high Herodian pitch and may have found the brilliant Herodias somewhat too fatiguing for daily companionship. But Antipas' wife was not so accommodating, being

*Teterrima belli causa.—*Horace*.

18

the daughter of the high-spirited King Aretas. She somehow got wind of what was going on in Rome, and when the happy pair had their arrangements about completed she had fled to Arabia, and her father's troops of wild horsemen were harrying the frontiers of Herod's dominions. Consequently the new bridegroom had to mount his steed and defend his domains. At present he is in his fortress Machærus, near the Dead Sea, and the fair enchantress is with him, to keep up his courage, I suppose. So I have written to Pilate asking whether I shall follow after Herod to deliver his letter or return to Cæsarea.

In the mean time I find Tiberias quite enjoyable, as I have met an old friend, Quintus Memmius Celer, in command of the Roman detachment which is stationed here. Besides, there are some interesting Romans and Greeks who have made themselves very agreeable to the nephew of the Procurator of Judea. There is, too, quite an amphitheater here, and I am told that the gladiators are not at all bad, and fight with considerable skill for provincials. As for dancing girls, you know the Orientals surpass the world.

Besides, I shall have a day or two to run up to Magdala, which is only some three miles north of here—a little village on the shore of the lake.

I got some tidings of the fair Magdalene, as well as of her prophet, in quite an unexpected fashion on my journey hither, which was by way of Nazareth and Cana. The former town is the native place of this Jesus, and I made some inquiries there about him. But his fellow-townsmen did not seem to think much of his powers. Some admitted that he had cured a few sick folk, and that he was a ready talker, a subtle interpreter of their sacred books, and a sharp fellow at an argument. They all thought, however, that he took entirely too much upon himself; and the idea that he—the son of Joseph, the carpenter, whom every one had known well,—could be the expected Messiah, the deliverer of Israel, was too absurd to be entertained by sensible men.

"Why, there goes his mother now!" exclaimed one of the Nazarenes, pointing to a middle-aged woman who just then passed us. "You can not see anything extraordinary about her, can you?"

I saw a mild, sweet face that still showed traces

of great beauty, but it was saddened by an expression I have not been able to drive out of my mind—an expression of infinite sorrow. Some one told me that she is of the ancient line of David, the greatest king of Israel, which may account for her majestic carriage as well as for her son's prodigious claims; while her face of sorrow may be caused by her seeing only too clearly what must be his ultimate fate if he persists in stirring up the people.

The next day at Cana, in the house where I had quartered myself, I found two of the Nazarene's disciples, whom he has lately sent out as deputy healers and preachers. The woman of the house presented to me her son, a fine-looking boy, whom she said they had healed that morning of a very hard fever by merely laying their hands on him and calling upon the name of their master. She is now a fanatical believer and would not listen when I suggested that the fever might have run its course, or that the medicines she had been giving might have finally taken effect. Had I been present, she said, I should have seen him grow well under their hands. Besides, she told me a queer story of Jesus' turning a lot of water into wine at a wedding here a year or so ago. She said she had tasted the wine and that it was excellent. What do you think of that, my Lucius?

When the two disciples returned in the evening from their preaching and healing tour about town, she begged them to preach to me. But they replied that they were sent not to the Gentiles, but to the lost sheep of the House of Israel. However, as I thought this was an excellent opportunity for finding out something definite about their master, I questioned them, and they, laying aside some of their stiff-necked Jewish pride, deigned partially to answer me. The readier talker of the two, who called himself Simon Bar-Jona, and whom his companion called Peter, is evidently the stuff of which rebels and fanatics are made. He has a thin face, large mouth, prominent nose, and bushy hair, but a pair of burning eyes that actually made me feel uncomfortable. His speech was quick and incisive. The other, whose name is John, is a quiet man of handsome features and noble bearing, and his winning smile and soft voice made me willing to listen to him even when I knew he was talking sheer nonsense.

I asked how they came to attach themselves to this carpenter.

"We were fishing," replied John, "fishing near our home, Bethsaida—I and my brother and Peter and his brother. The Master came to the bank and called us. 'I shall make you fishers of men,' he said, 'come, follow me.'—And so we followed him."

"Why?" I asked.

"We had no choice."

"And you have not regretted it?"

"Our life began when he called us."

Truly this Jesus must be a wizard. These men are as intelligent as the average Jew, who is the keenest man in the Orient, and yet, at a word from him they have left their means of subsistence.

"Do you think him the expected Messiah?" I asked again.

"Assuredly," replied Peter, his intense eyes fairly ablaze.

"How do you know this?"

UNDER PONTIUS PILATE

"Have I not seen the blind receive their sight, the deaf hear, the lame walk, the leper cleansed, even the dead raised up? Have I not heard from his lips words that no man ever spake before, words that have filled my heart with ineffable glory, with unspeakable love? He has changed me from a dull, ignorant fisherman into one who can speak words of truth, and heal the sick even as he does. Truly he is the Son of God, and he shall redeem his people Israel."

"But where will he raise his army? How will he overcome us—the unconquerable Romans?"

The fire died out of the eyes of Peter as he met my questioning look. He shook his head and murmured: "I am not sent save to the lost sheep of the House of Israel. Would you learn more, go and hear him."

Evidently, whatever plan this Nazarene may have, he has taught his followers some discretion, or else, what is more likely, he has not yet confided it completely to them. I tried to get something out of the milder John, but he gave the same reply as Peter. He seems as harmless as the dove, yet he may be as wise as the serpent.

24

THE DISCIPLES

Then I inquired about Mary of Magdala. They both knew her, and Peter blazed out again: "Truly, she is possessed of devils to think she can gain anything from our Master. She passed us with her train—scum of the earth—unclean dogs and Gentiles—and told John, who knows her family, that she was going to do homage to the Master. It will be a pretty homage she will pay—the Jezebel! How the Master will wither her with his scorn!"

"No, I do not think so," interposed John. "I know that she has many devils, but I know also that she has always been generous to the poor, and if she really listens to the Master, she will be saved."

"Saved?" asked I, "from what?"

"From her devils—and for the Kingdom of Heaven."

"The Kingdom of Heaven? what is that?"

"The Master will tell you. He says that he is come to bring it upon earth."

By this time I had had enough of these credulous inanities, and so I left them to their foolish selves.

UNDER PONTIUS PILATE

My freedman, Syrus, has just come in, and he
tells me that he has been to Magdala, and has
learned that Mary is at present abiding there. I
go this evening. Take care of your health.
Farewell.

III
The Magdalene

III

At Magdala

I KNOW you will hardly believe, my Lucius, what I shall write you—nor can I myself fully realize it yet; so I shall merely put down the happenings of this strange evening in their order. Perhaps it will clear my mind.

After the heat of the day was over I left Tiberias on horseback with Syrus and my centurion, Longinus. The sun was just sinking behind the hills when Syrus pointed out a large house on the outskirts of a pretty little village that hugged the shore of the lake.

"Are you sure that is the place?" I asked.

"I was told so this morning."

"Perhaps we had better ask this woman," I remarked, pointing to a slender figure seated by the roadside. She was dressed plainly and a veil concealed her face.

'Can you direct us to the house of Mary called the Magdalene?" I asked.

For reply the woman rose and drew aside her veil. It was Mary herself—and yet not herself. The beautiful features were the same, but the soul that looked forth from the deep, red-brown eyes was that of an utter stranger to me—it was so peaceful, so calm. She recognized me, however, and asked with a smile:

"What brings *you* here, Caius Claudius?"

I sprang from my horse. The hot words seethed up from my heart—but could not cross my lips. There was a strange something that seemed to hold her aloof from me—some barrier I could not pass. Had she been Cæsar's sister I could not have felt more timid. And yet there seemed to be no effort on her part to repel me. Her smile was full of sweetness, and her eyes looked into mine as fearlessly as those of a child. At last I managed to stammer out:

"I came to see you, Mary."

"Well?"

Was she acting a part?—or was she, having become tired of me, amusing herself at my expense? My anger rose. I thought of a bitter word, but I could not speak it. I could only ask in faltering tones:

"Have you forgotten the olive groves near Jerusalem, Mary?"

"Almost, Caius, my friend. All that seems like a far-off dream—or something that must have happened to some one else."

"I see it only too well, and feel it too," I replied, for the gulf between us seemed widening every moment.

"The demons have left me ——"

"And your adorers?"

"They too."

"But how?"

"It is the work of the Master, whom I follow and believe."

"What master?"

"Jesus of Nazareth."

"That mad prophet ——"

She raised her hand, and the words died on my lips.

"You will not say such things after you have seen and heard him. And—stay to-night in my house, Caius. To-morrow the Master comes to the seashore, where he will gather the multitude to heal and to teach them, and you shall hear him."

I agreed gladly, tho for another reason than Mary probably imagined, and ordered Syrus to give his horse to her. But this she refused, and we walked on slowly to the house.

After supper Mary sat and talked to me, but about nothing save the Master, his wonderful miracles and still more wonderful sayings. I remember she said something about his bringing to life the son of a widow at Nain, and something about loving your neighbor as yourself, but I was not listening so much to the words she was saying as observing in the flickering light the enthusiasm on her face as she spoke of the Master and of love. Certainly, this Jesus must be one of the greatest of wizards to so completely dominate such a wayward nature as that of Mary.

But here is the strangest thing! As she went on talking of love—every line in her beautiful being made for love, her eyes glowing with the tenderest light of love—I sat there stupidly listen-

32

ing, bewitched, my hands crossed in my lap.
Truly, not only has the Master driven out Mary's
devils, and made her his own, but he has surrounded her with a magic *aura* that keeps other
men's hands from her. I can not make it out,
Lucius. Not only is Mary utterly changed, but
something is the matter with *me*. I was a dolt,
a child—no man, no Roman at all—that such
a woman should affect me so. Perhaps some of
the Master's magic influence may have emanated
from Mary, and so have destroyed all my manhood. This is nonsense, of course, but I can not
understand it.

At the Third Watch.

After Mary left me, I wrote the above, and then
tried to sleep. But, tho my couch was of the
softest, I rolled and tossed about, the image of
Mary constantly before my eyes—as I had seen
her last beneath the olive trees near Jerusalem,
in raiment of cloth of gold and with the flames
of Eros flashing in her eyes. Before the calm,
sweet woman, who talked of loving every one, who
called all men her brothers, I, too, had been calm
and cold; but now, with this vision of the real

UNDER PONTIUS PILATE

Mary before my soul, the fires of love thrilled through me.

I recalled my first visit to her house in Jerusalem. I was brought by the son of the high priest, an advanced Sadducee, who entertains no foolish notions about Gentiles and defilement. There was a feast. What magnificence!—what lavishness!—what revels! And Mary ruled the disorder. An odd sort of respect was paid by all the noble debauchees to this magnificent hetaira who gave her favors where it pleased her wilful majesty. Then rose before my mind the wondrous day when Mary chose me, when the sparkling queen of the revels became the tender woman who loved—loved with all her passionate, clinging soul. Ah! the wondrous revelations! The insights into the heights and the depths of the human heart!—Angel and devil in infinite variety! I had never truly lived before.

I sat up on the couch and stretched out my arms into the darkness. Mary herself seemed to stand there in her shining raiment and glittering jewels, her red-brown eyes filled with a wavering, languid light.

THE MAGDALENE

"Mary! Mary!" my soul cried out as I sprang from the couch. But the vision vanished—I groped in darkness.

I could not return to sleep. I could not stay where I was. Perhaps this performance of hers to-night was but a passing fancy, one of those many changes that made her so enthralling. And as the image of the new Mary now rose before me in her plain garments and with that calm light in her eyes, she seemed far more desirable than when sparkling with jewels and with demoniac flashes in her glance. I must see her—see her and find out what she really was. And, remembering that

"Fortune and Venus befriend the bold,"*

I grasped my sword, and, having lighted a lamp, I sallied forth—the picture of Sextus Tarquinius, tho Mary, to be sure, is no Lucretia.

The first thing I did was to stumble over a little maid who was sleeping at Mary's door.

"Do not slay me!" the child screamed, terrified by my wild appearance with lamp and sword. "She whom you seek is not here. She is on the housetop."

*Audentem forsque Venusque juvant.—*Ovid*.

UNDER PONTIUS PILATE

The moon was shining brightly as I ascended.
By the parapet stood Mary, looking northward
toward Capernaum. On hearing my step, she
turned and said without the least surprise:

"So it is you, Caius Claudius?"

Again the gulf opened between us. The flames
of passion subsided fitfully. Finally I stammered:

"I could not sleep. I wished to be near you,
Mary."

"Poor soul!" This was not in mockery, but
in tones of genuine compassion. "Nor can *I*
sleep," she continued. "But I do not complain,
my heart is too full. Sit down by me, Caius. I
would speak with you."

"But talk to me about yourself; you are the
only thing I care to hear about."

"Very well, Caius. Do you wish to know how
I came to be what I am now?"

"By all means, Mary."

With clasped hands, and with her eyes fixed
upon the stars, she spoke as if to the empty air:

"It was in Jerusalem. I saw him as he went
through the streets. I heard his voice as he
blessed a little child by the wayside. I felt his

eyes as he looked up at my lattice. And then he passed on—out of the city. But his face, his voice, his eyes, never left me. They filled me with an all-pervading longing that was deeper than sorrow. My lovers tried to arouse me; but their faces seemed like the faces of madmen, their voices like the laughter of idiots, their eyes like the fires of Gehenna. Then I would rave and storm and sometimes sink my teeth into my flesh. And they would say that devils possessed me. Perhaps they did, for I do not believe the torments of Sheol exceed what I suffered again and again. At last my mind would not turn anywhere but toward him, the Master. I thought that perhaps if I went to him I might find favor in his sight—and—he might exalt me into his love—as—Solomon exalted the Shulamite. I knew well that I should suffer no more agony of longing if I could only see his face, and hear his voice, and feel his eyes, and—perhaps—he might lay his hands upon me too and—and bless me.

"And so, hearing that he was in Capernaum of Galilee, I came hither to my own house. Many of my lovers followed me. We were a right royal train—I, bedecked with gold and crowned with jewels, and they, attired in silks and fine linen. And on the way there was much revelry—for only then could I even for an instant cease to feel the eyes that had pierced my soul. But when the revelry was over—then—truly—then was there torture without measure.

"He stood by the sea, and the multitude gathered about him, and so great was the press that I could not come near him—but—still he saw me. I saw his face light up with a smile. I felt his eyes take possession of my soul,—I heard his voice saying—saying to *me:* 'Come unto me all you that labor and are heavy laden, and I will give you rest. Take my yoke upon you and learn of me; for I am meek and lowly in heart, and you shall find rest unto your souls.' And then he stepped into a boat, and his disciples rowed him along the shore, and the multitude followed.

"But I returned home, for I knew what I had to do. I sent away my followers and removed my rich raiment and jewels. They told me that he would sup that night in Capernaum at the house of Simon the Pharisee. I went up to the city. The feast had begun, and there were many people about the house to look at him as he lay at meat. And when I, pushing my way through the crowd, saw him, my heart overflowed with love, and, remembering the alabastron that hung about my neck, I entered, and flung myself down by the couch and kissed his dear feet and wept over them and wiped them with my hair and anointed them with the precious ointment. And he suffered me—because he knew—because he knew what I had in my heart. Then I heard him, talking with Simon, and Simon answered him. At first I could not hear what he was saying, because of my weeping; but at length these words came to my ears, 'Her sins which are many have been forgiven, because she has loved much.' And then, with his eyes turned to me, he said—and his voice was like a cooling spring: 'Your sins have been forgiven.'

"I rose to my feet, I clasped my hands; but I could not utter a word—the love and joy in my heart were too great. And after a little he said again: 'Your faith has saved you. Go into peace.'

"And now I am in the peace—the peace that passes all understanding. And my delight is to wait upon him, to minister to his wants. And I thank God that he has given me wealth enough to enable me to serve his Holy One whom he has sent to redeem his people Israel."

She rose and went down, leaving me on the housetop to gaze at the stars, and to wonder how this strange thing had come to pass between me and her. And truly I can by no means understand it.

IV
The Master

IV

At Tiberias

I HAVE seen, have heard the Master, and I shall try, my Lucius, to write down as nearly as I can what I have seen and heard. Write me and let me know what you think of it all.

At early morning we started for Capernaum. Mary would not take Syrus' horse, but rode on an ass, followed by some of her household, who carried with them a goodly store of provisions destined for the Master and his disciples. I made a few attempts to engage her in conversation; but, while she answered my questions with much sweetness, I could plainly see that her mind was fixed on something else. So I rode silent by her side, contenting myself with the view of her beautiful face. I could hardly bring myself to believe that this pure, even childlike countenance was that of the most fascinating and most famous hetaira in the procuratorship of Judea. And yet I must confess that her present beauty is far superior to that which had formerly enslaved my senses.

After we passed Bethsaida, we overtook an ever-increasing multitude hurrying along the road to Capernaum,—some on foot, some on horse-back, and some in litters or on rough stretchers.

"They are going to hear the Master," said Mary, divining my question, "and they are bearing their sick and infirm to be healed."

"But this is mostly a mere vulgar rabble. They will make strange subjects for your new King," I remarked.

"It is to the poor and to the afflicted in body and soul that the Master is come. The common people hear him gladly. The rich and happy do not care for his words, and they think that they do not need his aid; but we who have suffered, we who have known the body's pain and the heart's bitterness, we who labor and are heavy laden, we go to him and find refreshment and rest for our souls."

44

THE MASTER

"And you think him a great prophet, Mary?"

"He is the Son of Man, the Savior of Mankind."

There was no use disputing words said with such a tone of certainty; so I relapsed into silence, deeply moved by her absolute faith, and still filled with wonderment, not only at her marvelous transformation, but at my own equally marvelous alteration. To think that I, a Roman of fashionable life and Epicurean philosophy, a soldier of rank, a noble of the Claudian gens, should have spent last night as I had done, and should now be riding along beside a Jewish hetaira, who was probably playing at sanctification, —I accepting that pretense as real, and listening with close attention to her least remark.

As we drew near to Capernaum, the crowd on the road steadily increased until, in a place on the lake shore where the banks rose gradually from the water, we came upon a dense multitude. For a time our way was completely blocked by the surging rabble, which paid no more attention to me than if I had been a mere Galilean. I lost my temper.

"Make way for your betters!" I called out.

45

UNDER PONTIUS PILATE

"Out of our path, or I will ride over you." And I was about clapping spurs to my horse when Mary laid her hand on my arm.

"Caius," she said gently, "be calm. In the Master's eye we are all equal."

Would you believe it, Lucius, I became suddenly quiet like a chidden child, and meekly asked:

"Where is the Master, Mary?"

"He is not here yet. He will come from Capernaum either by boat or along the shore.—But, listen. What is that?"

From up the road came shouts and cries of jubilation.

"It is the Master!" cried Mary, flushing and breathing quickly.

Round the edge of a hill appeared a new crowd, cheering and dancing and singing. In the midst walked a dignified figure, followed by a group of some half dozen men. As they drew nearer I recognized among them Peter and John, and a dark, heavy-browed man that I was sure I had seen somewhere before.

"Who is that man, Mary?" I asked, pointing him out.

THE MASTER

Mary looked, then turned away with a shudder, but did not answer. Then I remembered. It was that Judas of Kerioth who had been so jealous of me when Mary showed me her favor. Syrus warned me that he was lying in wait to murder me—then he had suddenly disappeared, and now here he was, a follower of the Nazarene.

As the Master came abreast of us, I examined him more closely. He is of a good figure, like most of these Galilean peasants, and his features are of the regular Jewish type. At first sight he seemed to me in no way remarkable; but when he turned his eyes toward me, I forgot everything but the look in them that seemed to take possession of my soul. It was only with great difficulty, and by remembering that I was a Claudius, that I restrained myself from running to him like the rest of the multitude, who were crowding about, trying to touch even the hem of his garment.

"Mary," I heard him say, in a tone of inexpressible sweetness. "Come with me."

She sprang to the ground, and, trembling with joy, joined herself to his train. Just then I caught the eye of Judas, who glanced at me with a black look of hatred, which changed then into a smile as if of triumph. I can not comprehend what that man is doing in that company. Whatever may have attached him to the Nazarene, he is certainly not transformed like Mary; and it is not pleasant to think of his being so near her.

Every now and then, as the Master with his train pressed forward through the crowd, he would be stopped by those bearing some sick person. Then he would lay his hands upon the sufferer, lift his eyes toward heaven, and with a word or two would raise him to his feet. And the sick man would walk away as if nothing were the matter with him. I saw a cripple who had been touched by him throw away his crutches and go dancing down the shore to the great delight of the shouting multitude. It was really quite remarkable, and there is no doubt that the Master possesses extraordinary powers, wherever he may get them. I am sure, my Lucius, that even you would not be skeptical had you seen what I have, nor would you make any scoffing remarks, and say, "I can not like Apella, the Jew, believe it," as I did once.

The Master—for he really is a master of some-

48

thing or other—gradually made his way to a little mound that raised him above the multitude. There, surrounded by his special disciples, he completed his clinic before he began his oration. I remained with Longinus on the outskirts of the crowd, but sent Syrus to push his way close up to the mound, so that we should not lose anything that happened. From my point of vantage on horseback, I could see everything clearly, and, as my hearing is excellent, I do not think I missed anything that was said. When the last sick person had been healed, the Master came forward and raised his hand as in blessing. The vast concourse sat down in hushed expectancy. Just in front of him were Mary and several other women, evidently quite respectable, for I recognized among them the wife of Chuza, Herod's chief steward. These women, as if fascinated, kept their eyes fixed upon the Master.

In a soft but distinct voice he unfolded his teaching. I must say, my Lucius, that while he was speaking it seemed that everything he said was absolutely true—that all the suffering of this world was because men had not followed his doctrine. And his doctrine is extremely simple. Briefly it is this: God is our common father, and we are all his children—therefore brothers. The spirit of God is inherent in each one of us, and manifests itself through us. Universal love is the highest manifestation of this spirit which enfolds and cherishes all beings, and, if we would show forth this spirit truly, we too must love every man as we love ourselves. Therefore we should abjure hatred, envy, and strife, and also riches gained at our brother's expense, and we should devote our lives to the loving service of our fellows, whether rich or poor, high or low, good or evil. Then we should be perfect, he said, even as the Father in Heaven is perfect.

The Master encouraged his hearers to ask questions, and, during one of his pauses, a man came forward and begged him to speak to his brother, so that he should divide their common inheritance with him. But in a tone of sorrowful pity the Master replied: "Man, who made me a judge or a divider over you?" Then, turning to the crowd and apparently fixing his eyes directly upon me, as I sat on my horse raised above the rest, he went on: "Take heed and guard against the desire of riches, for a man's life does not consist in the abundance of what he possesses." And this saying, as nearly as I can recollect, he illustrated by the following parable: "The ground of a certain rich man brought forth plentifully, and he thought within himself: 'What shall I do, since I have no room to store my fruits?' And he said, 'I will pull down my barns and build greater; and there will I bestow all my fruits and my goods. And I will say to my soul: Soul, thou hast much wealth laid up for many years, take thine ease, eat, drink, and be merry.'" Just here I caught his glance full in my soul, and it seemed to say, Is this not true, O Epicurean? Then he went on, still holding me with his look: "But God said unto him: 'Thou fool! this night thy soul shall be required of thee; then whose shall be those things which thou hast provided?' So is he that lays up treasure for himself and is not rich toward God." And, turning away from me to his disciples, he continued: "Therefore I say unto you: Be not anxious for your life what ye shall eat, nor yet for your body what you shall put on. The soul is more than meat, and the body than raiment."

So strong was the effect of this tale on me that I dared not trust myself to remain there any longer, lest I too should be as bewitched as Mary, and, in spite of my wealth and position, my pride as a Roman and a Claudius, should go following him about the country. When the wizardry of his eyes was removed from me I felt as tho I had still some self-control, and so, telling Longinus to bring Syrus with him, I galloped back to Tiberias, not daring even to stop at Magdala, lest the witchery of *that* place should hold me there until Mary and the Master could come and complete my capture.

You may call this running away, my Lucius, and so it is; but a wise retreat is always better than certain defeat. When you have read some of the doctrines I was assenting to, you will say that I did wisely. Now listen—can anything be more insane in this wild world of ours, where "man devours man,"* than such a teaching as: "Resist not him that is evil; but if any one smite

* Homo homini lupus.—*Plautus*.

you on the right cheek, turn to him the other also.
And if any man sue you at law and take away your
coat, let him have your cloak also."

Just think of it! Where would be our great
Empire and its wonderful system of laws, had we
followed such doctrine! And note this: "Be not
anxious about the morrow, for the morrow will
take thought for its own things." Just imagine
the results to civilization if all men adopted such
a childish and improvident idea. I might give
you more, for the Nazarene's words stick in my
memory abominably; but I think these are enough
to show the utter impracticality of his teaching.
Far truer is Ovid's saying:

"Each one's pleasure is his own chief care," *

and this too, from wise old Plautus:

"To benefit an evil man, the danger is as great
  As if you were to wreak offense on one of good estate;
  And favor to the wicked shown reaps no reward but hate."†

Yet I must confess that it has taken all my

---

* Cura est sua cuique voluptas.

† Malo bene facere tantundem est periculum
Quantum bono male facere. . . .
Malo si quid bene facias id benificium interit.

53

philosophy, all my experience and worldly wisdom to meet and overcome the fatal madness caused by the Master's eyes and voice. When I hold myself down to cold reason, I can prove the utter folly in practise of these doctrines, however fascinating they may seem in theory; but if I let myself go for an instant and recall the look of the Master and the tones of his voice, I find myself saying: "Truly, if we were only to do as he says the world would be happy. It is all so simple— a child can comprehend it and live it—it is only our worldly life that is complex and out of joint. Why have mankind ever strayed from the true path?" and so on.

And yet the whole thing is insane, insane as Mary, insane as the multitude, insane as I shall be if I do not get that fellow out of my head.

Quintus Memmius Celer has invited me to a supper to-night. He promises me some gladiators that are excellent fighters, some dancing girls of great beauty, and some Syrian wine that he says is better than Falernian. I go in the hope that a bit of genuine life may wake me out of the hazy dreams suggested by that mad carpenter. "The

THE MASTER

brotherhood of mankind"—what folly! nay,
rather

> "Now is the time for mirth and dance;
> Wine and good cheer will joy enhance." *

Take care of your health, and I shall try to
take care of my wits.   Farewell.

> *Nunc est bibendum, nunc pede libero
> Pulsanda tellus.—*Horace*.

V
The Banquet

V

THE feast of Memmius was not a success, my Lucius, or rather I should say, one of his guests was not a success—at least, the guest and the feast did not fit each other. Memmius had made quite an effort, and the feast itself must have been nearly as good as the one Lucullus served Cicero and Pompey in the Apollo room. Better dishes and better wines I have never tasted, and the slaves who served us were handsome and knew their business. But that saying of the Master as he gazed into my heart kept ringing in my mind: "Thou fool, this night thy soul shall be required of thee." I could not silence it. The fatal thought took away all desire of gorging myself, so that I had absolutely no use for my emetic. As for drinking, I do not want to get drunk again after keeping sober through a whole feast and

59

watching the company, which at the beginning was a delightful group of witty Greeks and noble Romans and at the end as filthy a herd of swine as I have ever seen. Do not exult, my Lucius, I am not ready to become a Stoic yet; but I do see that there should be moderation in the enjoyment of the good things of this world. I believe Epicurus himself taught something like that. At any rate, one should not keep sober at a feast where others get drunk. To be the only sober man in a company is a most melancholy affair, fit to send a man to live with Diogenes in his tub.

But I should not blame Memmius; he knew me of old, and got up just what would usually have pleased me exceedingly. There was a gladiatorial combat that ought to have interested me. It lasted quite a time, with some skilful work on both sides, until the *retiarius* at last was cut down by a fine stroke. All the guests applauded the *secutor* vociferously; but, as I saw the young fellow's life-blood ebbing away, it made me feel a little sick—me!—who have cut down dozens of barbarians in battle, and have loved the circus from childhood! The reason of this was—another saying of the Nazarene had come into my mind: "Whatsoever ye would that men should do unto you, do you also unto them"; and for an instant I had imagined myself in the place of the dying victim—butchered to amuse a half-drunken company. As I said, it made me feel sick—so sick that I was obliged to leave the room until they had removed him and had wiped up the blood. No one asked me any questions when I returned—they probably thought I had taken my emetic, for they had been so busy stuffing and guzzling that they had not noticed my temperance.

Now tell me the truth, my Lucius; do you see any good in these combats? Is there not enough of bloodshed in extending and sustaining our Empire, and in keeping down the slaves and proletarians, without our forcing poor fellows to maim and slay each other for our amusement? I believe we should be brave and fierce enough without it. After all, those fellows are human beings just like us, and, had the turn of fortune been different, we might be in their places—butchered for their entertainment. I know you will laugh when you read this, and in fact, it is not very sensible; but truly, there is something in what the Master said that I have never thought of before, and which I must think out for myself.

When the company was pretty far gone in wine, the dancers entered. I must give Memmius credit for great taste, as the band was uncommonly beautiful and the dance evidently seductive, but somehow I was not fired or enthusiastic as usual. I compared coolly and critically the different styles of beauty and the varying grace of the postures. The rest of the company shouted their approval in unrestrained words, but as they were drunk it was easy to arouse their sensuality. Before the dance ended a feeling of disgust came over me. There was something revolting in the set smile that parted the lips of the dancers and showed their white teeth. It reminded me of the grin of a skull, while the large black eyes of the girls seemed to widen into empty sockets, and the clatter of the castanets was like the rattle of dry bones. I had to turn away my head to shut out the horrid vision, and yet I had drunk scarcely any of the Syrian wine.

THE BANQUET

The dancer that fell to my share when the wriggling and twisting was over was a large-eyed girl, Jewish type, with beautiful red-gold hair like Mary's. She spoke pretty fair Greek, and understood it perfectly, so I began jesting with her, and quoting all the lively verses I could remember, just to see how she would take them. She was not at all stupid, and even returned me some jests as good, if not better than mine. But all at once her lip quivered, and she turned aside her head—I think to hide a tear. As I looked at her in astonishment, another saying of the Nazarene came into my mind—something about a man not being defiled by what enters his mouth, but by what comes forth from it; for this comes from within, from the heart, and so defiles him. And I seemed to myself as bestial as the other swine.

Then, moved by a feeling of compassion, I talked kindly to the little girl, who turned her moist eyes on me with amazement, and I thought gratitude. So I got her to talk about herself. She said her name was Susanna, and told me the simple tale of her childhood, of the little peasant

63

hut not far from Bethsaida, and of how she played about the fields and on the shore, before her parents had been obliged to sell her to pay the tax-gatherer.

"When the man who had bought me came with his servants to take me away," she said, "father kissed me and ran into the house, but mother clasped me tightly in her arms, and I, too, clung to her, weeping and sobbing. We would not let go of each other, and so the men had to tear us apart, and as they carried me away screaming, I saw mother ——"

Here the poor little thing broke down and wept copiously on my shoulder. I knew it did her good, so I merely stroked her hair and said, "Poor little one!" in as sympathetic a tone as I could muster. Finally she lifted her eyes to mine. I saw in them the same look that is now in Mary's, and I also remembered a couple more of the Master's sayings, which, by the way, seem to crop up at the oddest moments. This time it was: "Blessed are they that mourn, for they shall be comforted, and, blessed are the merciful, for they shall obtain mercy." By this time I had gotten into such a state of self-contempt that I thought I would try an act somewhat in the Master's manner, to see if it would make me feel any better.

"Susanna," I asked, "do you enjoy this life?"

Her head sank back on my shoulder.

"Would you like to leave this place, and go back to live in the country as you did when a little girl?"

"How could I?"

"I think I can buy you."

The girl said nothing—she could not believe it—her lip quivered again in that pitiful way. I called out to Memmius, who still had some of his wits about him, as he is a regular amphora in his capacity for wine:

"Memmius, I have taken a fancy to Susanna. What will you sell her for?"

"I will not sell her, but you are welcome to her if you want her—she is not half bad. Keep her as a memento of this night."

I tried to get him to name a price, but he persisted, and so I accepted his gift—I shall send him one of my best horses,—that ought to make us even. Then it occurred to me that I should not keep the child—who clung to me as if she were

afraid some one would take her away—in such a
pigsty any longer, and, as the company were
now almost all asleep, I stole out with Susanna,
and we found our way home—sober, both of us.
I shall send the poor little thing to Mary. She
will know what to do with her—perhaps take her
to the Master.

Now, my Lucius, what do you think of that as
one of the nights of Caius Claudius Proculus?
I can not make it out myself. I am not sick, and
have not been ill a moment since I recovered from
the fever I had in Jerusalem a year ago. But,
whatever may be the cause, I am no more my old
self, nor have I been since my visit to Magdala
and Capernaum. It may be that the Master is
a real wizard, and has bewitched me with his evil
eye; for I can not get his words out of my head;
and as you have seen, they sometimes come up
in the nick of time, to influence my actions.
Between the purified hetaira and the inspired
carpenter, I am likely to lose all my manliness, all
my Roman virtue.

To make matters worse, what else do you suppose has happened? When I awoke the day after

THE BANQUET

Memmius' banquet, I called for Syrus. Longinus came instead and told me that Syrus had refused to come with him, but had followed after the Nazarene toward Capernaum.

"Perhaps," thought I, "he has noticed something that ought to be observed more closely, and has followed it up."

This Syrus is one of the most adroit rascals I have ever known. He is a regular mongrel cur—Syriac, Phœnician, and Jewish mixed, combining all the vices of these vicious races. I do not think he has a single virtue but one—his unswerving faithfulness and devotion to me. Here he again shows the mongrel cur. You know those dirty little dogs are absolutely devoted to any one who will overlook their nauseousness and pet them occasionally. Besides, he is a constant source of amusement to me. You, too, would have enjoyed him, had you come across him before you grew disgusted with our gay life in Alexandria, and, wrapping yourself in your Stoic solemnity, left me to keep up the festivities alone. I got him shortly after your departure and in rather a peculiar fashion.

67

UNDER PONTIUS PILATE

For a while I took as a companion in your place Quintus Cæcilius—I remember you disliked him exceedingly. I do not wonder at it, but I had no choice. He owned this Syrus and used to call him his jackal. Syrus deserved the name, for his scent for the finest game was marvelous. From the first he amused me, not only by his absurd sayings, but also by his ugliness; for his face is as ridiculous as a comic mask, especially when he splits it with his expansive smile. So I took an odd sort of liking to him. But he is an immeasurable liar, and the way he pulled wool over his master's eyes was atrocious, but so comical that I could never betray him.

One day, however, the stupid Cæcilius found him out and promptly ordered him to be scourged with scorpions. Syrus' agony of terror at the prospect made him look more ridiculous than ever; but, in the midst of my laughter, the thought came to me that it would be a shame for Cæcilius to torture the clever rogue for the very mendacity which had been used so often for his master's profit. So I offered to buy him.—You see, if I keep on, I am likely to become a slave trader

THE BANQUET

like Pomponius Atticus.—Cæcilius named a stiff
price—you remember how avaricious he is—and
I, because I had made the offer, paid it. A
moment after I felt that I had been, as usual, a
fool with my money, but truly I have never made
a better bargain. When Syrus saw that he had
escaped the torture, he kissed my feet and swore
that he lived but for me, that never, never would
he tell me an untruth;—and really, I believe the
rascal has kept his word absolutely.

A good chance for proving his devotion presented itself soon after. I got entangled in an
affair with the propætor's wife—I do not think
I ever told you about it—and it came near costing
me my life. She was a fine woman, but horribly
imprudent, so the propætor discovered everything, and set a band of assassins on my track.
They would certainly have got me, had it not been
for Syrus. As he has a lot of intimate acquaint-
ances among the subterranean population of
most of our large cities, he got wind of the plot,
and, going to the revengeful husband, offered to
betray me for ten thousand sestertia, also to lead
the band of murderers himself, so that no scandal

would be reflected upon the propraetor's noble household. The good man took the bait and paid over the cash, with part of which Syrus hired another band of bravos, and placed them in ambush for himself and the propraetor's rogues. The latter, under Syrus' leadership, walked into the trap, and were pretty roughly handled. The survivors fled, leaving most of their number on the ground, Syrus among them—he having dropped at the first onslaught according to a preconcerted arrangement. Then the rogue came and told me all about it. He also placed some six thousand sestertia—his profits in the transaction—with me to invest for him, and then suggested, that as he was reputed dead, it would be safer for him not to be seen in Alexandria, at least for a while. So he departed, and I with him—for obvious reasons. And, do you know, the rascal, tho he had risked his life in the affair, did not seem to think his performance in any way unusual. As I did not care to be so much indebted to a slave, I manumitted him. I must say that his usefulness has been greatly increased, as he can now do many things that would be impossible to a slave; and everything I set him to do, no matter how difficult, how dangerous, he seems to consider a privilege rather than a task. So when he appeared this evening and said that he had come to say farewell, you may imagine my amazement.

"Why, Syrus," I exclaimed, "what will you do without my protection?"

"I shall have mightier protection than that of Cæsar, even."

"What do you mean?"

"Master," he replied, "I am going to follow the prophet Jesus, who has come to redeem Israel."

"But you are not an Israelite?"

"I can claim it. My mother was a Galilean woman, and I am circumcised."

"And your father?"

Syrus did not answer, but smiled that beautiful smile of his, and went on as if he had not been interrupted:

"Jesus has come to redeem Israel, and he says that he is the Son of Man, and that our Jehovah has sent him."

71

UNDER PONTIUS PILATE

"How do you know that he speaks the truth?"

"Look at the marvels he performs. You remember how many he healed before he began to preach yesterday? And after you had gone he drove out devils from two fellows who were almost torn in pieces by them. You should have seen it. The devils, before they came forth, hailed him as the Son of God and begged him not to torment them, but they had to go anyway. Just think of that—the devils obey him and acknowledge him!

"After the preaching, I renewed my acquaintance with one of his chief disciples, Judas of Kerioth—you remember him, I suppose.—After all, when you know him better, he is a very fine fellow, an enthusiastic believer in the redemption of Israel, and in Jesus as the promised Messiah. He would give his life a hundred times over for the glorious cause, and, if he had half a chance, he would far excel his namesake, the terrible Gaulonite; for his sole dream is of the coming of the King of Israel, who shall rule the whole earth. Besides, he carries the common purse of the party —for they share and share alike—and he will undoubtedly be the treasurer of the new kingdom. So I made an especial effort to cultivate him, and I found him a very much sharper man than the others. He told me that the Master had sent them out a little while ago, having given them power to heal by the laying on of hands—like those two we met in Cana—and to command devils in his name. Judas asserts that he, too, has healed and has cast out devils—if I were sick he would show me what power he has, but, unfortunately, as you know, I am as sound as a nut.

"Then he told me a lot of wonderful things the Master has done. At Capernaum he healed the servant of the centurion Curtius—Longinus knows him—without touching the sick man or even going near him, merely saying a word when he was quite a distance off. And he raised the son of a widow at Nain, when they were carrying him out to his burial, likewise the daughter of Jairus, the ruler of the synagog. And the other day at Gadara, he drove out the devils from some half-dozen possessed fellows, and the devils asked him to let them go into a herd of swine that were feeding on a cliff near by. And he said, Go! and

the devils went and drove the herd headlong over
the cliff into the sea.

"And that is not all. He was out on the lake
the other day with his disciples in a boat, and a
fearful storm arose, and the waves beat into the
boat and nearly filled it, while all the time the
Master was in the stern, sound asleep on a cushion.
When they were just about to sink, the disciples
awoke him and cried: 'Master, do you not care
if we perish?' And he rebuked the wind, and
said to the sea, 'Peace, be still,' and, can you
believe it? there was a dead calm. Then he said
to his disciples: 'Why were you afraid? Have
you not enough faith yet?' And Judas says that
the Master has told them that when they have
faith enough, they will do greater things than he
has done.

"Just think of that! Think of the power I
can acquire if I follow him, the wealth I can amass,
the gay life I can lead!—and you shall share it all
too. Besides, the Master says that not only his
special disciples, but all who believe truly on him,
will not perish but will have everlasting life when
his kingdom shall come."

THE BANQUET

"Are you not a little foolish, Syrus?" I asked when he stopped for a moment to take breath. "What will become of his kingdom, even if he overthrow Herod? For then Cæsar will send his legions against him, and how long would that mob I saw yesterday stand up against one Roman cohort?"

"How long could ten Roman legions stand up against a King whom the winds and the waves and the very devils obey?" replied Syrus confidently. "As the angel of the Lord shattered the armies of Sennacherib, as the waters of the Red Sea swallowed the hosts of Pharaoh, so will the lightnings and thunders of Heaven scatter and destroy all those who dare to oppose our King; or he could order a legion or two of his devils to enter the Roman forces as they did the swine. Think of that!

"For that reason I came to you, my master. You know that I love you more than my own life, and I do not want you to perish in the destruction of our enemies. Go back to Rome, where you will be safe; or rather, come along with me and join yourself to Jesus. He will surely recognize your military skill, and make you chief captain of his army, for there is not a single one of his followers who can drill a troop. Just think of that!— Commander-in-chief to the greatest King in the world! Besides, with your influence, I might be put in charge of the commissariat, and you may be sure I should get out of it all that there is in it ——"

"I do not doubt *that*, Syrus."

"And all I should make would be at your service."

I laughed long and loud at his delusion. Then I was sorry, for I saw that he spoke from his love of me. So I talked kindly to him and told him that I too was anxious about his future. I also asked him whether it would not be better for him to wait a while until his prophet had gone from talking to acting. Then he could see if there were any likelihood of permanent strength in this new kingdom, and, in the mean time, I would take care of him as usual.

"No, master," he replied, "it is best that I go now while his disciples are few. There will be a better opportunity of my being noticed and my merits observed now than when he will be surrounded by triumphant multitudes. You see that Judas has already secured the best office of all, and, to get the commissariat, I must be stirring before others gain precedence. I am starting rather late perhaps."

"And you are going to risk *all* on an uncertainty?"

"It is no uncertainty. No one but a prophet sent from God can have such powers. And Jesus says, the Kingdom of Heaven is at hand. It is like a grain of mustard seed, that to-day is so small, but soon grows into a great tree giving shelter and protection to all who seek it."

"Do you want me to pay you that money I hold in trust?"

"By no means;—why?"

"You told me the disciples share everything in common."

"That is so—I had not thought of it." For a time he was silent. Then he looked up and said with a peculiar expression in his eyes: "I think you had better keep it—for a while, at least.— After all, one ought to be prepared for emergencies. I also have with me quite a little sum, and, if it please you, take most of this and put it out at interest with my other property in Gaul— or wherever it may seem good to you. I am keeping enough and plenty to put in Judas' purse if he should require it, for I should not like to join the prophet as a penniless outcast. And should I want any more I may draw on you, master, may I not?"

"Yes, Syrus, any time before your Son of Man raises the standard of rebellion. After that you must look out for yourself. And even if you leave him in time and get to me without being captured you will find me always ready to take you back; for I foresee it will be rather hard for me to get along without you."

Then the good Syrus, bursting into tears, fell at my feet, and protested that he would not leave me for any mere mortal; but this Jesus was certainly the long-expected Messiah, and so he could not, with his Jewish blood and faith, refuse to follow him now that he believed him sent from God. But, if I persisted in staying in Judea and did not perish with the Roman armies, he would see that I was preserved and even brought to honor before his Lord and Master, Jesus the Christ.

And so we parted. It will be some time before I can find any one clever enough to take his place.

This Jesus of Nazareth is certainly an extraordinary being if half what is told of him be true. From what I have seen with my own eyes even, he is a remarkable manifestation of more than human power. Perhaps the gods are awakening from their Olympian slumbers and are going to meddle in human affairs once more as in the days of Troy. I fear the plausible Epicurean hypothesis will have some difficulty in holding its own against such marvels. To think of the different people the Master affects so powerfully! There is Mary the hetaira, that fiery Peter, that gentle John, that somber Judas, that adroit Syrus— and I myself, a Roman citizen and soldier, a philosopher and skeptic, can not get him out of my mind.

Yet I do not like what Syrus says. In spite of all his peaceful talk this Jesus is evidently laying plans for some kind of a kingdom, and may be using his discourses of love and forgiveness as a blind for the authorities until he has the multitude completely bewitched. Should Pilate not order me to go to Herod, I think it would be just as well for me to stay here a while and observe how things are going. Of course Cæsar does not want to meddle in the affairs of the vassal kingdoms unless there be some certain danger to his empire; but then eternal vigilance is the price of victory. I should, however, personally prefer an order to go to Herod, which would remove me from the neighborhood of this wonder-worker. He has almost become an obsession with me. I dreamed of him last night, and I have not been able to get him out of my head all day. From time to time an almost irresistible longing arises in me to see and hear him again, and I sometimes wish I had some disease that he might heal me. Let me know, my Lucius, what is your opinion of this matter. Take care of yourself. Farewell.

VI
The Forerunne

VI

At Machærus

A S you see, my Lucius, Pilate sent me word to
follow up Herod, and so here I am in this
magnificent palace and impregnable fortress—
one of the masterpieces of Herod the Great.

Herod Antipas received me with distinction
and made me sit beside him as he gave audience. I imagine he does not care to leave an
offended Roman procurator behind him when
he goes forth to fight Aretas. And I do not think
he would have taken the least notice of Pilate's
little butchery of those Galileans in the Temple,
if he had not felt it necessary to do something to
keep his mad people quiet during his Arabian
campaign. He seems to me to be one of the
craftiest of foxes—handsome, insinuating, and
utterly unreliable—and makes me think of my
own good Syrus, whom, by the way, I have missed
exceedingly. I wonder how long the scamp will

be contented with wandering about in the train
of that mad carpenter.

But to return to my royal fox. He read Pilate's
letter immediately—his face absolutely non-com-
mittal—then overwhelmed me with a flood of
tributes to my uncle's many virtues and boundless
magnanimity. He was sure that everything could
be arranged satisfactorily, and invited me to
remain with him as long as I cared to. The very
next day he was going to celebrate the anniversary
of his accession by great games in the city, closing
with a feast in the palace to all his captains, and
he wished me particularly to be present. The
day after he would give me an answer that he was
sure Pilate would find satisfactory. Then, calling
one of his pages, he sent the letter to Herodias.
I have no doubt that she is the stronger character
of the two, and that in the end it is more Herodias
than Herod. For she is not only the descendant of
the great Herod, the Idumean, but, through her
grandmother Mariamne, of the still greater
Maccabees, those magnificent chieftains who
liberated Judea from the dominion of Syria nearly
two hundred years ago.

In order, I suppose, to still further show honor to the nephew of Pilate, Herod chatted with me for some time, keeping those who desired audience waiting. Finally there were announced two disciples of John the Baptist who wished to see their master.

"John the Baptist?" I asked Herod. "Is that the prophet who made such a sensation last year at the fords of the Jordan?"

"The same. Did you hear him?"

"Oh, no, I was enjoying myself too much in Jerusalem to want to go out and take a cold bath for my sins."

"You missed a fine thing. John is a magnificent orator—you have not any better in Rome —no one can excite a multitude as he can. If he had confined himself to preaching in the wilderness of Judea, and to stirring up the sluggish consciences of your Jerusalem Pharisees and Sadducees, I should not have imprisoned him; but when he transferred his *balnea** up to Bethabara and began catching my Galileans on their way to the high festivals, it became my busi-

* Public baths.

85

ness. I have little doubt that it was his influence that stirred up my people and got them into that riot which compelled the procurator to take such severe measures."

"That is quite likely," I assented, seeing plainly that this show of confidence was meant to impress me with his friendship for the Romans in general and for the family of Pilate in particular. "You think this John was planning a rebellion then?"

"Oh, no, not at all; his influence in that riot was indirect. He spent all his time and breath in denouncing sin and wickedness, preaching repentance and good behavior, and baptizing because the Kingdom of Heaven was at hand."

"What did he mean by that?"

"That the long-expected Messiah is coming."

"Was not that rather dangerous?"

"Oh, no! He did not claim to be himself the Messiah, but only his forerunner. When a man proclaims himself to be king or Messiah it is time enough to interfere; but a forerunner merely interests the people and helps to keep their minds off their own troubles."

THE FORERUNNER

"Do you mind telling me why you imprisoned him then?"

"Not in the least—and you may tell it to Pontius Pilate too, so he may see that in this I did him a service; for John finally did become dangerous."

"How was that?"

"He moved over across the Jordan into my territory, and got so puffed up with his success— he baptized hundreds and hundreds of my people —that, when I and my consort came down the Jordan on our way hither, he blocked our road, and dared—standing right before us, backed by his crazed multitude—to deliver an oration like that of your Cicero against Catiline. Tho he attacked me unmercifully on account of my pleasant little extravagances, I could not help admiring his oratorical style and the skill with which he shot his envenomed darts that took all my philosophy to parry; but, when he went on to abuse me on account of my marriage—right in Herodias' presence too—he became insufferable, so that there was nothing left for me to do but arrest him and bring him here a prisoner. Of course, his followers by hundreds surrounded this place and demanded their prophet. It was a regular Galilean mob—you know what that is—and, while I might have laughed at their beating out their silly brains against these impregnable walls, you see it would not have been good policy to make war against the Arabs and leave such a cause for disaffection and rebellion behind me. So—in spite of my consort's natural desire to have her insulter punished—John the Baptist, tho a close prisoner, is not badly treated. During the day he has the liberty of the upper citadel. I let his disciples see him whenever they ask properly and have been kept waiting long enough, and I tell them that I am only holding their prophet temporarily as a hostage for their good behavior and shall release him when my campaign is over— but what sort of a release I shall give him I have not yet decided," and as Herod said this I understood why he had been given the surname of "fox."

"He must be quite an interesting character," I remarked.

"Very interesting indeed. I have him frequently brought before me to preach and prophesy,

and, tho he is always offensive and his strange
sayings often perplex me, yet it pleases the people
that I hear him, and really, he is quite a diversion
in this dull place, where I must perforce wait
till Aretas attacks us; for I have no intention of
marching into the desert and meeting the fate of
your purse-proud Crassus."

"I should like to hear this John; you have
really aroused my curiosity."

"I will send for him, Caius Claudius; but no,—
perhaps this will be better. I have a lot of stupid
business to finish, and it may amuse you to visit
him along with his disciples. He preaches to
them in his very finest style so that they may report
to the rest of his followers."

I followed the guard along the massive wall
of the castle which is flanked by enormous towers
some ten score feet in height. We looked down
hundreds of feet on the city to the west, and
hundreds of feet up to the citadel perched like
an eagle's nest on the top of the steep eminence
to the east. It seemed as tho we should never
cease climbing the approaches to this perfect fortress that a whole army could not capture as long

as provisions lasted. The view from the summit was boundless. To the east and south, miles and miles of desert land; to the west, over the white walls of the palace and the roofs of the town, down for thousands of feet by successive steps to the Dead Sea, and then, across its heavy surface, to miles of wilderness closed in by the hill country of Judea, where one could even catch a glimpse of distant Jerusalem; to the north, the green oasis of Jericho, and the silver thread of the Jordan winding its way from the Sea of Galilee. As I stood viewing this broad outlook with admiration, the guard said:

"There is the prophet. But do not disturb him: he preaches best when you let him choose his own time."

I drew back and noticed that the disciples did the same. The prophet was certainly a strange-looking object—an immense, bony figure, clothed in a single rough garment, his rugged features surrounded by a tangled mass of jet black hair. He stood, his hands clasped before him, gazing out to the northwest, where such multitudes had hailed him as Master and Prophet.

Then I noticed, seated on the parapet and half hidden by his massive form, a richly attired young girl of great beauty, whose large, dark eyes were so intently fixed on the prophet that she did not observe our approach.

"Who is she?" I asked the guard.

"Hush! It is the princess Salome—the daughter of Herodias—let us retire." And he pulled the disciples back into the tower. But I, thinking it unfitting that a Roman officer should retire on account of a child, even tho she were a petty princess, remained where I was.

"And so you have no word for me, John of the Wilderness?" I heard her ask.

Then the prophet, still gazing into the distance, spoke in low, heavy tones like the roll of distant thunder:

"Behold the days shall come when the way of truth shall be hidden and the land of faith shall be barren. But iniquity shall be increased and the land shall be wasted utterly. The sun shall shine suddenly in the night and the moon in the day, and blood shall drop from wood, and the stone shall give his voice, and the people shall be troubled. There shall be chaos also in many places, and friends shall destroy one another. Then shall wisdom hide herself, and understanding withdraw into his secret chamber, and shall be sought of many and shall not be found. Then shall unrighteousness and incontinency be multiplied upon earth. One land shall ask another and say, 'Is righteousness gone through thee, or one doing righteousness?' And it shall say, 'No.' And men shall hope and obtain nothing; they shall marry and not rejoice, they shall labor, but their ways shall not prosper. . . . For the world has lost his youth and the times begin to wax old. And look, how much the world shall be weaker through age, so much more shall evils increase upon them that dwell therein. . . . For the grain of evil was sown in the heart of Adam from the beginning, and the fruit of ungodliness has been brought forth and multiplied unto this time, and shall yet be brought forth until the time of harvest come. And when commotion shall be seen in the world between the nations, and nations shall be disturbed, and the people shall be polluted, and princes shall hasten to mutual slaughter, and leaders shall be struck with consternation, then understand that of these the Most High has spoken as coming before his appointed time.

"And then shall come the Son of Man, to whom righteousness belongs, with whom righteousness dwells, and who reveals all the treasures of that which is concealed, because the Lord of Spirits has chosen him, whose lot before the Lord of Spirits has surpassed all through his uprightness forever. And the Son of Man shall drive the kings and the mighty men from their beds, and the powerful even from their thrones; and shall unloose the bands of the powerful with which they bind God's people, and break in pieces the teeth of sinners. And he shall hurl the kings from their thrones and their kingdoms, because they magnify him not, nor praise him, nor acknowledge with thankfulness whence the kingdom is lent to them. . . . And they shall be driven from the assembly of his church and of the faithful."

While John was still speaking, I stepped forward, the better to see his face. His rapt eyes were fixed on the western sky, where the sun was slowly sinking, flooding the air with golden light.

He did not notice me, but the little princess glanced in my direction for a moment and then again riveted her eyes on the prophet. After his last words, there was silence for a time. Then Salome, with a look that reminded me strangely of Mary of Magdala, asked:

"But tell me, you prophet, when your Son of Man comes, and has destroyed all the mighty ones,—what will he do with love?"

"With love? the love of God?"

"No, my wise prophet, the love of man—the love of man for woman?"

"I do not know it—nor is it worthy of a thought when the hour is at hand of the coming of the kingdom. Only repentance, only repentance shall avail."

"What is your repentance without love? what is life without love? Where would you be, where should I be without love—the gift of God? And *you* have not seen it." Here she slowly rose, laid her little hands on his broad shoulders, and looked straight into his eyes. "O you blind prophet, you blind prophet, wrapped in your foolish dreams! Here have I come day after day, have

listened to your voice, have heard your wondrous
words—they have consumed me as with fire—and
my eyes have gazed into yours and have told you
all—all—all. But you have seen nothing. Come
now, look away from those distant heavens, and
gaze deep into the heavens of my eyes. Tell me
what you see there. Look, O John the Prophet,
and tell me what you see there—tell me—if you
dare!"

John turned his firm look toward her languish-
ing gaze; then, without a word, without a change
of countenance, put her gently aside, and once
more contemplated the glowing horizon. The
little princess, with a petulant toss of the head,
turned from him and suddenly became aware that
I was not a common soldier of the guard, as
she had probably thought, but some stranger of
rank. In an instant her features hardened, the
childish beauty vanished, her dark eyes glowed
aflame. With tightly clenched hands she stood
again before John and hissed through her set
teeth:

"Listen, you foolish prophet. He who knows
not love will soon know—hate; for hate grows out

95

of love, which is the center of its being. Go back to your empty visions and dream as long as you can."

Then, paying not the least attention to my presence, she called her maidens, who had been waiting some distance off, and began the long descent of the citadel. She looks like the rest of her intense and vicious race.—But what a strange thing it is that she as well as her stepfather should be so taken with this wild prophet! Perhaps it may be his very exaltation and aloofness, the superb virility and rugged power she can not tame. Still I fear that the prophet's days will not be long, since he now has two such women as Herodias and Salome hating him. Of this danger he probably thinks little or nothing; for, as she departed, he looked after her with a weary but compassionate smile. This changed to one of gladness, as he saw the guard advance with his disciples, who knelt at his feet to receive his blessing. As they arose he asked:

"And you saw Jesus?"

"Yes, Master. We found him near Capernaum, surrounded by a great multitude, bringing many sick and infirm people whom he healed. We asked him the question you charged us with, 'Are you he that should come or do we look for another?' And he answered, 'Go your way and tell John the things which you have seen and heard: the blind receive their sight, the lame walk, the lepers are cleansed, the deaf hear, the dead are raised up, and the poor have the good tidings preached unto them, and blessed is he who shall find no scandal in me.'"

"And what were the good tidings that he preached?"

"Master," said one, "I can not remember all that he said, but the thought was this: All men are brothers, they are all the children of the same God, and their first duty is to love one another. That was the burden of his speech. 'A new commandment I give unto you,' he said, 'that you love one another. As I have loved you, so love you every one, even those that harm you, even the Gentiles and the sinners.'"

"Yes," added the other, "I remember he said, 'Love your enemies, bless them that curse you, do good to them that hate you, and pray for them

that despise you and persecute you; that you may
be the children of your Father who is in heaven;
for he makes his sun to rise on the evil and the good,
and sends rain on the just and the unjust.'"

"And his face beamed with kindness, and
warmth filled my heart whenever he looked at
me," continued the first; "and surrounding him
were publicans and sinful men and sinful women,
all gazing at him with love. Numbers of children,
too, were brought to him that he might bless them.
They crowded about him, the little ones, and
when some of his disciples would keep them back,
he said, 'Suffer little children to come unto me
and forbid them not, for of such is the Kingdom
of Heaven.' And he took a little child and set
him in the midst of them and said: 'Except you
become as this little child you can not enter the
Kingdom of Heaven.' What did he mean by
that, Master?"

While the disciples were talking, John stood
with downcast eyes, and now when they ceased
he did not answer; but the thoughts chased each
other across his face like clouds before a tempest.
At last his somber features lighted up, as with the

great light that comes when a storm lifts at sunrise, and he spoke exultingly:

"I see it all now! It is he that should come—the Son of Man—to redeem Israel—no, not Israel alone, but all the earth! And I was so blind that I was looking for another, so blind that a little wayward girl could tell me of it—seeing more clearly than I—I, who thought myself a prophet. Truly I am not worthy to loose the latchet of his shoes; for he is the light of the world, the sun who shines on all, and asks not if they be worthy or unworthy. And I knew not love, only hate, hate of sin and wickedness, a hate that would destroy the wicked utterly like a black tempest. Truly my hate was so dark, so dense, that it shut out the sun, the sun of love, that blesses everything; because it sees that offenses must come; that were there no evil there could be no good, were there not sorrow there could be no joy, were there no strife there could be no victory. And when we see this, we can do naught but love. The offender must suffer because of his offenses, but we must love him and aid him because of his suffering—not turn away because of his offenses. Verily, we must become as little children, for they love and love simply, with no question of worth or unworth, good or evil. O Lord of Spirits, I thank thee that I have seen the light of love and have beheld thy beloved Son in whom thou art well pleased. For he is the Messiah, the Christ, the Holy One who shall redeem the world—Jew and Gentile, the righteous and the sinner, by his infinite, eternal Love. In hate is death, but in Love is life everlasting! And now," he concluded, turning to his disciples and pointing to the Sea of Galilee, "the Bridegroom has come and the wedding feast has begun with joy and love and thanksgiving. I said once that he must increase and I must decrease, and now I say that my work is done. Go you to the Bridegroom and rejoice with him in love. Leave me here to await what the Lord will send me—of good or of ill, it matters not, for my eyes have seen the coming of the Kingdom of Heaven."

VII
Temptation

VII

At Machærus. Midnight

I STOPPED writing, my Lucius, because word was brought by a page that Herodias wished to speak with me. I found her in her private room with the princess Salome beside her. She recalled our meeting in Rome, and was even more affable than Herod had been. We talked about indifferent things, tho I plainly saw that her mind was on something else, and that she was looking for a way to introduce it. Finally, as if spurning indirection, she came straight to the point.

"What did John the Baptizer say to you?" she asked.

"Nothing," I replied.

"Did you not go to hear him?"

"Yes. I heard him prophesy to his disciples, and a little before that I heard him speak in another strain."

Here the little princess gave me a quick glance from her dark eyes, as if to enjoin secrecy upon me. I smiled and was silent.

"So you did not speak with him?"

"No."

"It was just as well. He would have offended you deeply; for he has a bitter tongue and is no respecter of persons. What did he speak about?"

"Of the sins of the world and of the coming of the Messiah."

"That is all he can talk of except when he is abusing some one. Had you spoken to him he would certainly have preached about *your* sins, and those of the divine Cæsar. I can not see how such a coarse fellow should so influence people. Why, Herod likes nothing better than to listen to his tirades, and even little Salome here loves—"

"Hush, mother!" interrupted the girl, "do not speak of him again. I hate him."

"What?"

"Yes, I hate him!—hate him!—hate him! I do not want to see him or hear of him again." The beautiful features hardened, and the deep eyes flashed a hatred that needed no words.

TEMPTATION

Over the handsome face of Herodias stole a smile of content, and, as she stroked her child's hair, she looked like some superb tigress caressing her cub.

Just then Herod entered. Herodias went to him and laid her arm affectionately on his shoulder. It is plain that these two are devoted to each other, and in their royal fashion make no concealment.

"Herod," said his wife when he had greeted me, "Salome can entertain our guest for a time, for I need to consult you immediately about quite an important matter."

As the curtain fell behind them, Salome, who had for some time kept her eyes on the floor, looked up and said with a laugh:

"Come over here, Roman, and sit beside me. For *I* want to consult you immediately about quite an important matter."

"Well?"

"Then what did you think of the things you heard and saw on the citadel?"

"I did not think. You are a princess, and may do what you choose."

"Oh, you wise Roman! You are even wiser than the prophet John. And you seem discreet, able to hold your tongue. I like the look in your eyes, it seems honest. Now, you wise Roman, can you be honest with me? Can you keep a secret?"

"I swear it. What then?"

"I must confide in some one. You say I am a princess and can do as I choose; but I can not make people trustworthy. I have no one to confide in."

"Your mother?"

"Not in this matter. And as for Herod— hush!—he loves me dearly, but I can not trust *him*. But I feel I can trust you. Besides, you are going away in a few days, and that will end the whole matter. And then—what you saw saves me telling you much that it would blister my tongue to utter." This strange mixture of childish frankness, precocious wisdom, and subtle charm astonished me, and I watched her with ever-absorbing interest as she went on. "I do not know what it is that draws me to you, my wise Roman; but I feel certain you are the one I need.

TEMPTATION

Come now—be honest with me.—You did not
think anything about me? Then what did you
think of the prophet?" And she watched me
slyly out of the corners of her long-lidded eyes.

"The prophet? He is marvelous."

"There! I knew you were honest. Did I not
say so? If you had not been honest you would
have answered differently. But truly the prophet
is marvelous. He has bewitched the whole of
Herod's household, like a serpent that fascinates
before it strikes. Herod is fascinated every time
he hears him speak—he never would have imprisoned him had it not been for my mother.
And mother is fascinated too—that is why she
hates him so. I never understood mother's
hatred till to-day. But now I understand—
only too well. And you, O wise Roman, saw how
I was fascinated—" Here she turned away
to hide the blush that overspread her face and
bosom. But when she leveled her dark eyes
once more upon me I felt them penetrate me
through and through. She will certainly be far
more dangerous than her mother when she grows
up. That Asmonean stock is wonderful. "Yes,

I will tell you all," she continued, laying her little hand on mine, her look changing to one of perfect childlike confidence. "When I first heard the prophet speak, my soul was as tho transformed. All the greatness and the terror of the earth and of the heavens surrounded me, and I was uplifted as by angels to behold the destruction of the whole world. Little of it could I fully understand, but I could listen to him forever. Why this was so I can not explain—I only know it *was* so. And then, as my mother would not allow me to hear him when he preached to Herod, I used to steal up to the citadel and listen to him, as you saw. But as the days passed, what he said, tho it was still beautiful and terrible, tho he himself grew still more terrible and beautiful, yet something was lacking. My heart cried out, and there was no reply. He did not say the word I longed to hear. And to-day—Oh! how I hate him!—hate him!—hate him!"

She looked me straight in the eyes, her dark orbs flashing like those of a tiger, in the intensity of the fury that possessed her as she thought of how the prophet had scorned her—in my presence. The innocent, confiding child had vanished, and in her place writhed a passionate, beautiful demon. My blood was deeply stirred, but I answered as calmly as I could:

"I understand. But what do you want of me?"

"Ah! you understand. I know you understand. And, since you understand so well, do I have to tell you what I want? The daughter of Herodias never forgets—and—she can reward richly." Her glowing eyes were now close to mine, and the half-parted crimson lips, whose sweet breath I could feel, told me, more plainly than words, what that reward might be. But I sat silent, looking with wonder upon this strange being, half child, half Lamia.

"Speak," she cried impatiently. "Is it possible you do not understand? Have I made a fearful mistake?" She drew back a little.

"No," I replied. "You have made no mistake. You want me to kill John the Baptist. But how can I, a guest in Herod's house, slay his prisoner?"

"Listen," she said. "You have been already to hear him. You can go again. He stands near the parapet. He speaks vehemently. You are angered—you, a Roman—that a slave should so address you—the fall is many, many cubits—and Herod could not hold a Roman ambassador accountable for one dead Jew—and I ——"

It was my turn to draw back—shocked by the treacherous depths in this young girl.

"Child," I said, "I am a Roman, a soldier. I could not do such a thing."

She looked at me in blank amazement.

"Then you have never slain a man?"

"Often; but in fair, open fight, when he could defend himself. Get your prophet to stand up against me, and I will fight him for your favor."

I can give you no idea, my Lucius, what a weird fascination this little minx possessed for me—so young—almost childish—so wicked, so treacherous. But I imagine she comes by it naturally, as she is the daughter of a grand-daughter of the great Herod by one of his many sons, and the inbreeding has concentrated in her bewitching personality all the striking traits of this lurid race. For some time Salome was silent, evidently thinking, but all the time keeping me fixed by her languid eyes and the enticing smile of her scarcely parted crimson lips. Then leaning over, and laying her arm on my shoulder, she whispered in my ear:

"I have the plan now. This John is a Judean, and belongs in Pontius Pilate's jurisdiction. You can claim the prisoner as yours. Herod will not dare refuse, or rather, I think he will be glad to have him taken off his hands—and, then—on the way to Jerusalem—one of your soldiers—now, do not shake your head—you need not make the arrangement—I shall do that—it will only cost me a trifling jewel or two—but the jewel I will give to you will be beyond all price—and——"

At that instant she sprang away from me. "Get back into your old seat—quick!" she whispered.

"What is the matter?" I asked as I obeyed.

"It must be some twenty miles to Jericho—at least so I have been told," she said, as Herod and his wife pushed aside the curtain and entered the room.

"You must pardon our absence, Caius Claudius," Herod said, "but Herodias is planning a special feature for the celebration to-morrow and wants it to be a great success. I really think we can show you something as good as you have seen since you left Rome. But we well know that we have nothing here that can compare with the Roman Circus."

A slave now announced supper, which I was asked to take with them as sole guest. At table Herodias entertained us with amusing incidents of her various visits to Rome, and even gave some comical traits of the divine Augustus, who used to play with her when she was a little slip like Salome. I can well imagine how she hoodwinked the old Divus Cæsar. What a witch she must have been! Something like her daughter who sat there now so quiet and demure that no one would ever dream that, but a short time before, she had been plotting a treacherous murder. But every now and then, when it was safe, she would flash a swift glance at me as if to remind me that we were accomplices. There is a fascinating subtlety about these Orientals, my Lucius, that we Romans have never possessed, and which far transcends the keen insight of the Greeks.

TEMPTATION

Shortly after I had retired to my chamber, I heard a light tap on the door. I opened it, and saw in the corridor—Salome,—her feet bare, and a cloak thrown over her head, covering all her face but her glowing eyes.

"Come in," I cried, holding out my hand.

"Not yet, my wise Roman," she laughed, as she shrank back. "You might have asked for the Baptizer to-night at supper; but you missed your chance. You are slow, my Roman, and the race, you know, is to the swift."

"I am swift enough to catch you," I cried, endeavoring to seize her. But she eluded me easily, and, knowing that I would not pursue her far at that hour, she presently returned, and with the wickedest look imaginable on her childish face, she whispered:

"To-morrow is your last chance, O Caius Claudius Proculus—and if you miss that you will be more stupid than the Baptizer himself. Good night." And in an instant she was out of sight.

She is certainly an amazing creature, this mixture of childish frankness, devilish treachery, royal dignity, and reckless abandon. I can not get her out of my head, and so have sat up to write this to you, hoping to ease the tension of my being by a sort of confession. But the little minx may be sure of one thing—she will never get me to be her tool in such a dastardly plot—not even if she possessed ten times as many charms.

VIII

The Daughter of Herodias

VIII

At Jericho

HERE, in the quiet of this beautiful city, my
Lucius, I shall finish the tale of my adven-
tures with the Herods. I must admit that these
Oriental royalties with their intense natures and
treacherous plots, their rapid changes from passionate love to deadly hatred, are more than I,
modern tho I am, can bear. I believe I still have
some of the old Roman virtue in me. You may
remember that my mother's name was Porcia;
and I like to think that some trace of the noble
Catos may yet abide in my blood.

I confess, however, that the Catonian blood,
if there be any left in me, was tremendously disturbed by that little witch Salome. I slept little
after her flying visit. In my heated imagination
I continually saw her as she sat on the parapet,
her large eyes fixed on the prophet, her whole

soul absorbed in him. I could not help thinking what a fool he had been to scorn her and that his death would be no more than a just retribution. But, tho I would have given a great deal to be in the place he once held in her strange little soul, I could not quite bring myself to the idea of occupying it by any such treachery as she had planned.

At sunrise I left my uneasy couch, my mind still being tossed by the conflicting winds of desire and honor, and went out upon the palace roof that I might refresh myself in the cool air of the morning. Above me towered the massive citadel, dark and gloomy except the summit, which was glowing like a beacon in the first rays of the sun. I saw two figures appear on the parapet, one a soldier, the other unmistakably the prophet with his scanty garb and disheveled hair. He turned his face to the north and stretched forth his arms toward the Sea of Galilee, then toward the rising sun, and then, with bowed head, walked back into the tower.

As I descended into the palace, I met the princess, who beckoned me to come to her.

THE DAUGHTER OF HERODIAS

"Hush!" she whispered, "I have been looking for you. I only want a word, and Herod must not know that we have talked together. Now listen. Do not ask him for the Baptizer till after I have appeared at the banquet to-night."

"Why?"

"Because—you will see then. Perhaps I shall not need that plan."

"Are you going to forgive John?"

"I must not linger here any longer; but you will see—and remember—the daughter of Herodias never forgets an injury or a benefit." And with a glance that was full of promise she sped away.

The games given in the new circus were excellent. The gladiators were not at all bad—some capital cuts and slashes being given—and there was one *retiarius* who trapped and slew the *secutor* in an exceedingly skilful manner. The lions were better than those we have in Rome. They are captured in the desert near here, so their spirit is not broken by a sea voyage and too long confinement. The magnificent leap that one of them made, bearing down two slaves at once,

would have done your heart good; and so delighted were the spectators that he was given his
prey to finish at his ease in the cage. As for the
chariot races, there are no horses like the Ara-
bians, and the best of the breed were contending.
The drivers, too, were as reckless as you could
wish, and there was quite a thrilling collision near
the finish of the first race. One of the chariots
dashed by another, taking off its wheel, and
throwing the driver against a column, which
dashed out his brains pretty thoroughly. The
disabled chariot with its plunging team swung
round directly in front of two others that were
close behind, and in an instant all three were in a
beautiful tangle. When they got things straight-
ened out, the chariots were tolerably well wrecked,
another driver was dead, his back broken, and
the third had both legs shattered, besides being
well sliced about the face and chest. Two or
three of the horses had to be killed—which was
a great pity, for I have never seen finer animals.
In fact, I may say that I enjoyed the circus as
much as ever, and it made me smile to think that
in Tiberias I had felt sick on seeing a single

gladiator bleed. But associating with these Herodians has been a good antidote to the poison of the Nazarene. I am getting to be my old self again.

During the games, Herod had me sit at his right hand—I suppose, to show the people that he was on excellent terms with the Romans, and that rebellion would be dangerous. On his left was Herodias, and at her feet Salome, who from time to time glanced up at me as if again to remind me that we were accomplices—tho Jove knows I never at any time agreed to her dastardly plot. Still she acted as if I had, and I must admit that I was strangely moved whenever her eyes met mine.

The banquet that closed the day's festivities was superb. Herod has become so completely Romanized that I doubt whether outside of the divine Cæsar's palace anything better could be provided, and the Syrian wines are certainly delicious. All the captains of Herod's army and the chieftains of his auxiliary forces were present. I reclined in the place of honor on the breast of Herod. On the other side of him sat Herodias, who directed the serving of the feast. She was gorgeously attired, her magnificent body being almost encrusted with priceless jewels, which glowed and flashed in the wavering light of the torches. When the last meats were removed, and the revel about to begin, Herodias arose and addressed her husband:

"Mighty sovereign," she said, "it is but meet on this glorious anniversary of your royal accession —the first since you took me as consort to share your magnificence—that I should contribute something to your honor and to the entertainment of these your friends and followers; and I could think of nothing more worthy than that my own flesh and blood should appear before you for the delight of your eyes. Permit therefore that I retire to prepare this pleasure for you." And with great dignity she withdrew behind the heavy curtain.

Then to the sound of harp and flute slowly floated in the little Salome herself, attired in a diaphanous robe, her hair, bosom, arms, and ankles ablaze with jewels, her eyes glowing with the flames of Eros. Her dance was similar to those you and I saw so often in Alexandria; but there was one great difference—this was danced by a princess, one of the most enticing princesses in the world.

As she swayed there before me, my head swam in a sea of dizzy desire, I felt that I was willing to do anything she might ask, and I was even thinking how I might frame a request for the prisoner John, when I heard Herod's soft and penetrating voice:

"O daughter of Herodias, you are the greatest glory of my reign, the greatest treasure of my realm, the greatest honor of my feast, and truly I can find no words to praise you. But—ask whatever you will—and I will give it to you. Yes, I swear it unto you. Whatever you may ask of me, I will give it you, unto the half of my kingdom."

I looked at his face. There was no drunken light in his eyes as he made this extraordinary offer; but he glanced over at the curtained door, and there, between the half-parted folds, I fancied I saw the face of Herodias.

Salome stood silent as if appalled at her success;

then she asked timidly if she might consult her mother, and, when permission was given, disappeared quickly behind the curtain. It seemed but an instant before she came forth again As she stood before us she shot a side glance at me, a mysterious glance that I could not then fathom, and then in a diffident tone she said:

"Most mighty Herod—may it please you—to give me—forthwith—on this charger—the head of John the Baptist?"

Herod hid his face in his hands and moaned aloud.

"Will you not ask anything else, my child? Choose some of my richest cities. Yes—even as I said—half of my kingdom."

"No, mighty lord," replied the little princess, her tone growing bolder as she proceeded, "I want nothing but the head of John the Baptist —on this charger. And nothing else will I take. No, not even your whole kingdom. You have given me your royal oath, and you can not disavow it without dishonor to yourself, and to these great men about you. I hold you to your oath, and I will that you give me the head of John the Baptist."

THE DAUGHTER OF HERODIAS

"You have spoken truly, O daughter of Herodias," said Herod after a silence. "I have given my royal oath, and tho it grieves me to slay that great prophet whom I love, yet for the sake of my royal honor, and for these that sit at meat with me, I shall not deny you." And he ordered one of the guards to bring the head of John.

Not a word was spoken while we awaited his return. Herod covered his face with his cloak. Once again Salome glanced at me, smiled triumphantly, and then looked away indifferently. I understood it all now—I was no longer needed. The whole scene had evidently been arranged by Herod and his clever spouse to save him with the people, she being perfectly willing to bear the whole responsibility. Salome must have been taken into the plot late at night or early in the morning; but she, probably fearing that Herod might weaken at the last moment, had determined to keep me as a sort of second string to her bow in case the first should break. Now that her arrow had hit the mark she could cast me aside. As you may imagine, my pride suffered, and suffers yet; but I know that I suffer this sting because I toyed with the little serpent, when I should have repelled her first dishonorable suggestions. Still, as I looked at the shifty Herod, hiding behind his cloak, I was glad it was my pride that was hurt and not my honor.

The guard returned with the bloody head; the eyes stared threateningly, while the livid lips were parted, as if to curse. Herod turned away his face to avoid the sight; but the maiden, taking up the great dish in which the head had been brought, bowed and said:

"I thank you, O mighty Herod, for your right royal gift." And then she bore it to her mother, who issued from behind the curtain. Herodias received the ghastly burden from her child, elevated it as in triumph, and with great dignity passed out.

We all breathed more freely when the curtain fell behind her; but the joy of the revel could not be revived. The shadow of death —not the death of a slave or a gladiator, but that of a great soul—had settled upon us and we could not shake it off. Some tried to jest, but the laughter died upon their lips, and at an early hour we separated, mournful and sober.

Early this morning I received Herod's answer to Pilate's letter, and tho urged to stay longer, I had no intention of meeting the mocking eyes of the little minx of a princess, and so departed.

To-day those two disciples of John, who brought him the message from Jesus, passed through the city with his body, which they had begged from Herod. They had tried to get the head from Herodias, but she sent them word that she had thrown it to the dogs. They were also told by the slaves that she had thrust a bodkin through the tongue of the dead prophet, had spat in the face, and had reviled the head as if it were alive. Many other disciples of John were following his body. When I asked them what their plans were, I was told that they were going to bury the body in a tomb belonging to his family, and then they would obey his last charge and join themselves to Jesus.

I think I shall remain here for a few days; I feel wearier than I should, and a little rest will

do me good. Take care of your health, my
Lucius, and write me one of your good letters.
Let me have one of your truly philosophical discourses, something noble and Greek,—I have
had enough of the Orient for a time.   Farewell.

IX
The Multitude

IX

At Jerusalem

I ARRIVED here, my Lucius, just before the Passover, and as I entered my quarters in the Tower of Antonia, who should come to meet me but Syrus!

"What brings you here?" I exclaimed. "I thought you were going to serve the new King of Israel, and be one of his chief lords."

"So I was," assented Syrus with great coolness as he began to remove my travel-stained garments, "so I would be now, were he the man I thought he was. But I follow no one who will not avail himself of his own powers, and use his opportunities as they arise. I believe in men, not children, and the Nazarene's kingdom may be fit for children and women, but it will not do for men. I certainly believe, that as he says, a man must become like a little child if he would enter his

131

kingdom; therefore his kingdom is not for *me*.
Let him fill it with babes and women and fools;
I must serve a master I can respect."

"But, Syrus, are not his powers genuine? Did
you discover any trickery in the miracles he
wrought?"

"None at all, and that is the worst of it. His
marvelous powers are real, whether they are from
God or from Beelzebub; but he does not know
how to use them any more than the babes he
admires so much. But, if you wish, master, I
will tell you all that happened after you departed
till the time I left him—I am happy to say without
leaving any of my money behind me, so that all
I have lost is a little time from your service."

"Tell me everything, Syrus. It will help me in
making my report to Pilate."

"Well, master, the day you left, I returned to
Capernaum, and found the Master. By this time
all the disciples whom he had sent out had returned and reported what miracles they had
wrought. And each one brought quite a crowd
in his train. And there was gathered about the
upper end of the lake a great multitude of

THE MULTITUDE

Galileans, who were going up to Jerusalem for the Passover, and did not wish to go in small parties on account of the incursions of the Arabs, which you know are quite frequent now. So they had gathered together in a large body, over five thousand in number besides women and children, and many of them were well armed, and they were going to travel the shorter road through Samaria. Now these people, hearing of the wonderful cures Jesus had done, crowded about him, bringing as usual all their sick and infirm, and insisted on his healing them. Jesus, after working over them for hours and healing every one, at last took refuge with his disciples in an upper room in order to have a little quiet. But a lot of Scribes forced their way in to dispute with him, and a set of daring fellows clambered up to the top of the house, broke in the roof, and lowered a paralytic, right down in front of him. Instead of kicking the dirty fellow out of the window, the Nazarene first said that his sins were forgiven him, and then told him to take up his bed and walk. The fellow was a withered wreck and the cure was marvelous; but I did not like the way the crowd forced their way in on the Nazarene. A real leader, a true king, having such powers as he possesses, would have made the dirty rabble keep their distance and show him some respect."

"But, Syrus, how did you get close enough to see all this?"

"Oh, I pushed my way in right after the disciples. I kept close to Judas and got ahead of the mob."

"To show your respect to the Master, I suppose?"

Syrus is no fool, and catching the gleam in my eye, smiled one of his beautiful smiles.

"Do not be too hard on me, master, just because I have been a little foolish and have been misled by my enthusiasm. But honestly, I would have given to Jesus of Nazareth the highest respect and even worship, had he been worth it. I tell you that if he were only better able to appreciate men like me and Judas, he might even now be sweeping this land from end to end, the greatest king on earth."

"It is lucky for me and my uncle and the divine Cæsar that he did not appreciate you—eh, Syrus?"

THE MULTITUDE

"Have mercy on me, master," he said with another smile. "But truly it was almost pitiful. He got completely exhausted with his preaching and healing, and the strangest thing was that he never seemed to think it worth while to use his wonderful power on himself. I asked him why he did not relieve his own exhaustion, and he said something about the Son of Man suffering for the sins of the world. Do you know, I believe that he likes to suffer, and actually enjoys a headache. When at last he was totally fagged out, he got into a boat with his disciples and rowed across the lake beyond Bethsaida Julias, leaving the crowd gaping on the shore. Judas told me that he would try to get me into the boat as one of the oarsmen, but I refused. I did not want this great multitude of men to lose sight of the prophet, and start off to Jerusalem without him. The thing to do was for the prophet to enter Jerusalem at their head as the leader of an army, and then, by a few of his miracles, take possession of the citadel."

"By Hercules, Syrus, what a dangerous rebel you are! I believe I shall have to hand you over to Pilate."

For a moment Syrus was alarmed and grew deadly pale. Then, seeing I could not keep the twinkle out of my eye, he smiled again and continued:

"No, master, you should rather reward me as a deserter who brings important information. Well, as I was saying, I could not let him lose his hold on this great multitude, so I hurried about among them, and told them that as the boat was crossing against a contrary wind, we could, if we made haste along the shore, get to the other side before him. So, starting out with a few of the most enthusiastic fellows, I soon had the whole crowd in motion, and as they went I hurried up and down suggesting that now was the time for the prophet to proclaim his real mission, now that he had so many magnificent men ready to do his bidding. They took to the suggestion like fishes to water. Well, so rapidly did we hasten, that the first of us got to the landing-place in time to welcome the Nazarene ashore, while the rest of the mob came straggling after, the women and children bringing up the rear. Some of them had been made ill by their exertions, and so Jesus had to begin as usual by healing them. But his rest on the boat must have revived him, or he may have worked a little miracle on himself, for he seemed just as fresh as ever, and preached in a wonderful manner.

"I can not remember half what he said, and there is much of *that* which I can not understand, but, while he was speaking, it seemed God's own truth, and I was more than ever sure that he was the Son of Man who should redeem Israel.

"Now, as evening came on, some of his disciples interrupted him and suggested that he send the multitude away, so that they could go into the country round about and buy something to eat. You see I had got a place in the front rank and could hear everything. And what do you think the Master said? 'Do *you* give them something to eat.' The disciples answered, 'Shall we spend two hundred denarii for bread to give them to eat?' And he said, 'How many loaves have you? go and see.' And one of them, Andrew, Peter's brother, replied, 'There is a lad here who has five barley loaves and two small fishes; but what are these among so many?'

137

Well, this did not disturb the Master in the least, and he said cheerfully, 'Make the men sit down.' So there we sat down, as we were bid, in companies of about fifty each, not one of us having the slightest idea of what was going to happen. And now comes the wonderful part. You never could imagine what he did. He made his disciples borrow baskets from the crowd, and then he took the five loaves and the two little fishes, and, looking up to heaven, he blessed them and gave thanks and broke them and gave them to his disciples to distribute to the crowd; and, as fast as one basket was filled, he started in with another and—— "

"Now, look here, Syrus," I exclaimed, "you are asking too much of me to believe this. You said there were five loaves and three fishes—— "

"I said five loaves and two small, very small fishes; and no matter how many baskets were filled, there were the five loaves and the two fishes in front of him. I saw it as plainly as I see you, and may God strike me with leprosy if I lie."

"You mean to say that he fed five thousand men with five loaves and two fishes?"

"Yes, more than five thousand. There were

138

CHRIST FEEDING THE MULTITUDE, from the painting by Murillo

"He took the five loaves and the two little fishes,
and, looking up to heaven, he blessed them and gave
thanks and gave them to his disciples to distribute to
the crowd."

a hundred companies of fifty each—I counted them myself—and a great crowd of women and children besides, and when they were all satisfied there were fragments enough to fill several baskets."

"If this be true, your Nazarene is the most remarkable wizard I ever heard of."

"It is true, and if he were only a man like you, and knew how to use his powers, what might he not do! I was so anxious to see how he did it, that I too borrowed a basket, and came up and got it filled; but, tho I stood right in front of him, I could not find out. He just went on breaking and breaking, and when my basket was filled, there was still something before him with which to fill the next. I could not help thinking then, what a wonderful commander he could be, and how easily he could handle an army—no baggage train, just a single basket of food, and they could go anywhere. And you remember that woman in Cana told us he had turned water into wine. Just think of it! Think of the wealth I could accumulate if I could only get some of his power! Well, as I passed among the men, distributing the food, I kept saying to them, 'Here is our leader. Let him be our king. No matter where we march we shall not hunger; if we are wounded he can cure us, if killed he can raise us from the dead. With him we can conquer the world.' And they all agreed with me."

"I wonder the Nazarene did not see it as you did, Syrus."

"He would have if he had had any sense. I even went up to him after all were filled, and told him that he only needed to say the word, and we would proclaim him King of the Jews."

"And what did he say to your kind offer?"

"He looked me through and through, and, tho I tried hard to stand erect and look him straight in the eyes, I felt as tho the ground were giving way under me.—I tell you, master, that man has wonderful power."

"I should say he has—to abash Syrus Bar-Sarah; but did he say nothing?"

"He spoke in a soft, even sad voice, and said, 'My time is not yet come. Watch and pray lest you fall into temptation.' And then I stammered out something about my not being to blame, that

the crowd was quite determined to have him for
their leader, and, in fact, I heard behind me murmurs of 'Let Jesus be our King,' and 'He is the
Holy One of Israel.' And Jesus heard them too,
and turning to his disciples, he bade them go back
across the lake in their boat, and said he would
dismiss the multitude, and then would remain
by himself for prayer.

"So the disciples rowed off, and Jesus told the
crowd to go and find resting-places for the night.
But they began to murmur and cry out, 'We will
have Jesus for our King.' And I, slipping back
into the mob, called out, 'Now is the appointed
time. Whether he is ready or not, let us make
Jesus our King.' And the crowd shouted, 'Jesus
of Nazareth, King of the Jews,' and began to
move toward him. Then I saw him grow pale
as a ghost, and he raised his eyes toward heaven
and moved his lips as in prayer. And then—
you may not believe it, master, but—he was gone;
where, I do not know; but we stood there fool-
ishly looking about for him. Some said he had
sunk into the earth, others that he had flown
through the air, others that he had slipped through

the crowd. But, anyhow, he was gone—we could find him nowhere. So, finally, seeing that he was a wonderful man, and thinking that he might know the proper time for assuming his kingship better than they, the crowd dispersed, some to the villages round about, while others slept out on the grass.

"As for me, I could not sleep, but climbed about the hills in the moonlight, looking for Jesus. I thought if I could only find him alone, I could declare myself his true disciple, and perhaps he might teach me some of his magic knowledge— at least he would learn to know me as an individual, and I should not be just one of the 'multitude.' You know I have learned a lot of military science and business being with you, master, and I was going to tell him all about it—— "

"You would make a capital general, Syrus," laughed I.

"Anyway, master, I could have done much better than any of those foolish disciples or those wild tho brave Galileans—— "

"How would you set about organizing an army, Syrus?"

THE MULTITUDE

"Do not jest with me, master, but let me go on with my story. After a long search my diligence was rewarded. There on the top of a hill, which sloped almost perpendicularly into the lake, stood Jesus in the attitude of prayer. I slipped behind a bush to wait till he had finished his devotions, knowing that the only practical path down the hill led past my hiding-place. He prayed for an interminably long time, and when he had ended, instead of coming down to me, he turned and went over the cliff! I sprang to the edge and looked over. There he was, standing on the narrow strip of beach and looking out over the water. I followed the direction of his gaze, and thought I could dimly see a boat in the distance. And then, the next moment—now this is the solemn truth, master,—he was walking out over the water just as if it were dry land."

"Syrus, did the Nazarene give you anything to drink when he fed you?"

"Not even water. And Judas told me the next day that their boat was out in the middle of the lake, kept back by contrary winds, and that Jesus nearly frightened them to death, when they saw him coming to them over the rolling waves, for they thought he was an apparition. But the Master called out, 'Be of good cheer. It is I! be not afraid!' And Peter, who is always boiling over with enthusiasm, answered and asked if he could go to meet him. And Jesus said, 'Come,' and Peter started out all right. But when he felt the waves splashing about his feet, he got frightened. Then immediately he began to sink, and called to Jesus to help him, which he did and got him safe into the boat. The Master told him that if he had not doubted, he would not have sunk. Now what do you think of that?"

"These are the greatest marvels I ever heard of. But how in the world could you ever leave such a thaumaturge? He might have taught you how to make bread without flour, and to walk dry-shod on the water, for I am sure, you brazen rascal, you would never doubt your power if you were once fairly started. How *could* you leave him?"

"I will tell you. It was the next day. When it became known that Jesus, as well as his disciples, was on the other side of the lake, those of us who had money to spare crossed in the boats that had come over looking for passengers, and the rest went back as they came. We found Jesus preaching in the synagog in Capernaum, and, pushing our way to him, we asked him when he came there. And he replied, 'You seek me, not because you saw signs, but because you ate of the loaves and were filled.' Then he said a great deal more, and of much of it I could understand nothing, but I remember pretty clearly the most absurd part, for I can not get the stuff out of my head.

"It was something about not working for the meat that perishes, but for that which abides to eternal life, and which he could give us. He said that his Father gave the true bread that came down from heaven and gave life to the world. And we cried, 'Lord, give us this bread always.' And now just imagine what he said! 'I am myself the life-giving bread. Those that come to me will never be hungry, and those that believe on me will never thirst. I have come down from heaven, not to do my own will, but the will of my Father who sent me; and his will is this—that every one who sees the Son and believes on him shall have enduring life, and I, myself, will raise him from death on the last day.'

"I am quite sure those were his exact words— they stuck in my mind on account of their strangeness. As you may imagine, the Galileans did not take to them very kindly. I heard some say, 'Is this not Jesus Bar-Joseph, whose father and mother we know well, and how can he say that he has come down from heaven?' And tho Jesus heard this, he went on insisting that he was the living bread come down from heaven, and whoever ate of this bread should live forever, and that this bread was—his flesh.

"Here a number of us protested against this revolting saying, but he kept on repeating; 'My flesh is true meat, and my blood is true drink. And those who take my flesh for food, and who drink my blood,' he said, 'are always in union with me, and I with them. As the living Father made me his messenger, and as I live because the Father does, so those who take me for their food will live because I do.'

"At this the murmuring became louder. Even

some of his disciples said: 'This is a hard saying; who can bear to listen to it?' And then the Nazarene asked, if this caused us to stumble, what should we think if we saw him ascending up to where he came from? And he added that we were all looking for mere material signs: that his kingdom was not an earthly kingdom, but a heavenly kingdom—not material but spiritual. 'It is the spirit that gives life,' he said; 'mere flesh is of no avail. The truths I have been teaching you are spiritual and life-giving; yet there are some of you who do not believe them. That is why I told you that no one can come to me, unless enabled to do so by the Father.'

"Well, this was too much for us, and pretty nearly every one left the synagog. I think only his twelve chief disciples remained with him. You see it was one of two things: either his teaching was horrible and impossible, or it was as figurative and visionary as the obscurest of the prophets. If everything was to be spiritual and the flesh was to amount to nothing, then farewell to all hopes of a kingdom that would amount to anything—and the flesh amounts to a great deal with me, as you well know, master.

"Then some of the Scribes and Pharisees came and talked to us, and said that Jesus allowed his disciples to pluck grain on the Sabbath and to eat bread with unwashed hands, and that when they had protested, he had replied that after all, it did not make much difference how or what a man ate, for no man was defiled by what he put into his body. At this all of the crowd who were going up to the Passover, not wanting a king who would set aside the law and tradition, departed for Jerusalem.

"So that superb material for an army passed out of his hands. And consequently, when the news came that John the Baptist had been beheaded, Jesus thought it best to leave Herod's territories and go into Syro-Phœnicia. Just think! if he had only let that band of Galileans proclaim him king, he could have marched on Herod and properly avenged the death of his forerunner. But, as it was, he had to take refuge in another country, and let all his fine preparation go for naught.

"I saw Judas just before they started, and he told me that, after the crowd left, Jesus asked the twelve if they also wished to leave him. But

Peter, with his old enthusiasm, answered that the Master's teaching led to eternal life, and that they had learned to believe he was the Holy One of God.

"'But, Judas, do you still believe?' I asked. 'I do,' he replied, 'tho his present conduct is a sore trial to me. Yet, as there have been many things that I have not understood at first but have become clear afterward, so I shall still follow him and hope; for I know that he is no ordinary man.'

"However, I did not relish the prospect of dodging about through those heathen lands. I am not interested in what the Master calls the spiritual things—they are too hazy for any one with common sense,—but I only wish I could have learned how to make bread and wine, and to command those devils. It is a shame that the Nazarene is so impractical."

"So you have come back to me then?"

"Yes, if you will take me, master. You arc at least a man."

"And you consider nothing human foreign to you," * I laughed, as I told him to make himself at home.

* Et humani nihil a te alienum putas.—*Terence* (altered).

149

UNDER PONTIUS PILATE

I am exceedingly glad that Syrus has returned, for I have missed him greatly. He is very like his namesake in Terence's *Heautontimoroumenos*, a perfect rascal, but absolutely indispensable.

To my report on Jesus of Nazareth, I added many things from Syrus' tale. Pilate agreed with me that there was little or no danger to the province from such a prophet. In fact, as he preaches a doctrine of non-resistance, it would not be a bad idea to encourage him a little. My aunt Claudia was greatly interested in what I said, asked me a lot of questions, and expressed a strong desire to see the Nazarene.

But he did not come up to the Passover, or, if he did, he kept himself well concealed. And, thanks to the strong force Pilate had in Jerusalem, and perhaps to the effect of John the Baptist's death, everything was quiet during the feast. Yet I hear there is great dissatisfaction in Herod's realm over the prophet's execution, for the people thought very much of him, and I fear that Herod will still have trouble about the matter.

In a few days I return to Cæsarea to see about getting several cohorts ready for a campaign, as we expect trouble on the southern border on account of Herod's war with Aretas. I shall return with the troops to Jerusalem in time for the Feast of Pentecost, which occurs in about a month. Take care of your health, my Lucius. Farewell.

X

The House of Love

X

At Jerusalem

HERE I am, my Lucius, back in the capital for the Feast of Pentecost. During the last month I have been very busy with military preparations, but nothing happened in Cæsarea that you would care to read about, and so I did not write. Something has happened here, however, that I think will interest you. That clever rascal, Syrus, since his return seems determined to make me feel that he is indispensable. He is everlastingly putting himself out to serve me, and this morning he appeared, his face wreathed in his customary smile, and asked:

"Master, are you still interested in the Lady of Magdala?"

"Certainly, very much indeed. So she is in the city, and you know where she is?"

"Of course. I should not have mentioned

her if I had not exact information. Shall I conduct you to her house, or shall I bear a message for you?"

The contrast between the serene face of Mary, as I had seen her last at the feet of the Master, and the vicious countenance of that little minx, Salome, as she danced in Herod's hall, rose in my mind; and I felt a strong desire to see how Mary's penitence had lasted. You know:

"Woman is always uncertain and changeable." *

"I think, Syrus, you had better go to her first and ask if she will receive me," I said. "Her attachment to the Master may have been more lasting than yours."

"Most likely," rejoined Syrus with a grin. "The Nazarene completely bewitches the women —they all lose their wits over him. But the Lady of Magdala has been back in Jerusalem quite a time, and she is not following him about the country any more. You may find that she has taken in a new set of devils, livelier than the first lot."

"Hold your impudent tongue and bear my message."

* Varium et mutabile semper fœmina.—*Virgil.*

THE HOUSE OF LOVE

In a short time Syrus returned with the reply that Mary would receive me at any time I chose to come, and so I had him conduct me to her dwelling.

It was a small but well-kept house in a respectable part of the city, very different from the magnificent abode she had formerly occupied. I was ushered in to the court and found Mary sitting by the fountain, conversing with a fine-looking young man whom she presented to me as her brother, Lazarus. She told him what I had done for the little slave girl, Susanna, and that I had heard the Master preach. This interested him very much, as he had come to believe in the Nazarene, during one of his visits to Jerusalem, even before his sister had been won over. He talked much of the Master, repeating many of his sayings with profound reverence and in an extremely convincing manner. Unlike the case of Syrus, it is the spiritual aspect of the new kingdom and not the material wonders, that has won his allegiance.

During our conversation a kindly looking but not beautiful woman came into the court, and

Mary presented me to her. She was the elder sister, Martha. Martha would not sit down, but bustled about the house, apparently very busy. She would occasionally stop and listen admiringly for a few moments when Lazarus was talking, and then would hurry away to give some order to the servants. But what impressed me most was the beautiful and affectionate way that both Martha and Lazarus treated the fair and formerly frail Mary. You would never suspect, on seeing the three together, that one woman had once been the most diabolically enticing hetaira in all Jerusalem, the other always the most respectable of Jewesses, and the young man one of the strictest of the Pharisee sect. The new commandment of the Master, to love one another, is certainly obeyed in this house.

After a while Lazarus departed and I was left alone with Mary. But I had exactly the same feeling as at Magdala. While she was not in the least offish, she seemed to be surrounded by a certain atmosphere of purity that kept me at a respectful distance.

"I have not seen you, Caius," she said, "since

158

you rode away so hurriedly when the Master was preaching by the sea. I should have thought you were offended, had it not been for what little Susanna told me about you and your kindness to her. But what did you think of the Master?"

"He certainly did impress me deeply that morning by the sea," I replied, "and it was owing to one of the things he said that I sent Susanna to you. But there were many things that I did not understand."

"You will understand them in time, Caius. They will keep coming up in your mind, and when you think them over often they grow clear."

"I fear I have been too busy to think them over much."

"As the Master says," Mary remarked sadly, "the thorns of this world have sprung up and choked the good seed of life. But may I ask you what has kept you so busy?"

"My mission to Herod, and some military affairs."

"So you saw Herod? Did you learn anything definite about the death of John? You know all sorts of stories are current."

159

I told her then about my stay in Machærus, omitting, of course, all mention of the little episode with Salome.

"John was a wonderful man," she said, when I concluded. "I heard him preach once. At first I was deeply stirred, and then he repelled me. He had no tenderness—he knew not love— and it was love alone that could give me peace. But John did a great work; he prepared the way for Jesus, whose kingdom is Love, and I am glad to know that John recognized it before he died."

"Tell me about the Master, Mary. Were you with him when he fed the five thousand men?"

"No, that was on the other side of the lake; I was in Capernaum then, but John, the disciple, gave me a full account of it, and also of the Master's walking on the water. Have you heard of that?"

"My freedman, Syrus, saw it."

"I must talk with him about it. Yes, the Master did many wondrous things at that time; but it was not the miracles that made me believe on him. It was not what he did, it was what he said— nay, rather, it was what he is, that won me to him.

THE HOUSE OF LOVE

To be near him is peace inexpressible, to hear his voice is joy unutterable, to feel his touch is life eternal."

Her face was illumined as by a light from another world. I saw that I was absolutely forgotten in the vision she had called before her. And, Lucius, it seemed to me that for the first time I saw what truest love is. It is no blind "madness of love,"* as we have been accustomed to figure it, but a calm, exalted surrender of one's whole spiritual being to the object of adoration. I was so moved that for a time I said nothing—Mary, looking into the distance, and I, gazing at her transfigured face.

"Did you," I finally asked her, "hear those sayings in the synagog of Capernaum, that caused so many of his disciples to fall away?"

"Yes, I was there."

"Can you tell me exactly what he said? Syrus tried to, but he evidently did not understand the Master."

"No, Caius, I can not—there is much that I too do not yet understand and perhaps never shall:

* Insania amoris.—*Ovid.*

but I know it is all true—because he said it. For he is the Son of the living God, and is sent to bring us eternal life. Every now and then his beautiful words float through my mind like angels from heaven—I hold them for a while and dream upon them, and am filled with a peace that passes all understanding. But often when I try to tell some one else, I choke, and the words will not be uttered. I once asked the Master why this was so, and he said, 'In a little while you will know me fully, in a little while the Comforter will fill you with the Holy Spirit, and that which is turbid will be made clear, and that which is hidden will be revealed.' O Caius, I wish you had stayed longer and had heard him again! You are better able to understand him than I, and you surely would have believed. But you must hear him again. He has promised to visit us at the Feast of Tabernacles—that comes in the autumn,— and you, too, must come and be with him."

"I shall try to," I replied. "But, Mary, how did you come to leave him and return here?"

"The Master sent me. He said he should be

obliged to wander about and tarry in no city, that he would often have no place to lay his head, and that we women must not follow him. As for me, he told me to return and be reconciled with my brother and sister. And when I said I feared their scorn and contempt, he smiled and said that he would make the path clear for me. And you have seen that he kept his promise. What a blessed thing love is, it suffers all things, it endures all things, and is kind! Ah! how good every one is! How good is our Heavenly Father!"

Then she sat silent again; but now it was she that spoke first.

"Caius," she said, "I have been very remiss in not telling you about dear little Susanna. I had search made for her parents and discovered that her father had died and her mother had gone away with a soldier. So I took Susanna to Jesus and he blessed her, and she believed, and ever since she has been so happy, so anxious to help every one, so glad when she has done anything for another."

"Keep her, Mary. I give her to you; for you only can understand her."

"I thank you for your gift," said Mary simply. "Let me call her."

When Susanna came, I could hardly recognize in the modest, pure-eyed maiden, the voluptuous dancer of Memmius' feast. She thanked me without affectation for what I had done for her. Then Mary said:

"Susanna, Caius Claudius has given you to me as a present; but I can not bear to think of my little sister as my slave, so now you are free, and you can go where you will."

The girl's face lighted up with joy at the word "free"; but then she burst into a torrent of sobs and tears.

"You do not—you can not mean that I must go away—must leave you," she cried. "No, no, I should be lost again—no, no, I should die!"

"No, dearest," said Mary, as she put her arms about her, "I meant you were really free; but if you want to stay with me, no one shall part us."

Susanna buried her face in Mary's bosom. At this moment Martha passed through the court, and Mary told her what I had done. Martha's hearty joy was good to see. I think, my Lucius,

THE HOUSE OF LOVE

that it is quite likely the Kingdom of Heaven the Master is trying to found has even now come upon earth, and is in actual existence in the abode of Lazarus, Martha, and Mary.

They asked me to remain to supper with them, which shows how thoroughly they are emancipated from the Pharisaical superstitions. And, as I left them, these words, "The peace of God that passes all understanding," kept running through my mind.

Syrus has just come in with the news that Herod sent forth his army to meet Aretas, and has been totally defeated, losing almost his entire force. He says that everybody declares that Herod's defeat was the result of his murder of John the Baptist. How the proud Herodias must suffer when she thinks that she alone may be the cause of her husband's bitter humiliation,—or at least if she does not believe what the people say, it must be hard for her to know that they think she is the evil star of the man she loves. And little Salome? I wonder if the Master could change her as he has changed Mary and Susanna?

This defeat of Herod, however, is going to keep

us pretty busy in Judea; for, even if Aretas has sense enough to keep out of the Roman territory, there are sure to be marauding bands of his wild horsemen who will slip over the border for the sake of plunder. Well, I should not mind some right lively fighting now. I fear I am getting morbid with all of this wonder-working, prophesying, preaching, and loving. But I hope I have some Roman manhood yet left in me.

By this time there ought to be awaiting me in Cæsarea your answer to that first batch of letters I sent you—that is, if you have thought as much of me as I have of you during the past few weeks. I am sure that some of your calm, cool, why not say frigid Stoicism, is just what I would most relish at this moment. Keep yourself in the best of health, my Lucius, if you love me. Farewell.

XI
The Stoic

XI

*Lucius Domitius Ahenobarbus in
Athens to Caius Claudius Proculus in Cæsarea of Judea sends
greeting*

THE first five of your letters, my Caius, relat-
ing your mission to Tiberias, came to me
in one bundle on the ship *Golden Wings*, which
arrived in the Piræus last night. I read them
immediately, one after another, with ever-increasing interest, to the end, and am now awaiting
with impatience the arrival of the next bundle,
which I hope will come from Machærus. I have
heard much of that fortress, as my father knew
the great Herod well and used to tell me many
tales of the adroit and merciless policy by means
of which he managed to pass safely through all
the entanglements of our civil wars. I am also
quite anxious to learn what sort of a man his son
has become, for I too was acquainted with him
in Rome.

UNDER PONTIUS PILATE

Your letters brought before me that strange Orient so vividly that for a moment I almost wished I had followed your example and entered the army. But when I began to reflect calmly I saw that the course I have chosen is the most suitable one for me. In this corrupt and degenerate world a life of philosophic retirement and scholastic poverty is the only course by which a man can possess his own soul and follow the straight and narrow path of virtue. In a calm retreat one can alone feel the breath of the Eternal Spirit, of the Infinite Father from whom all gods and men proceed. And to one who has once felt the inspiration of the Everlasting Spirit, the noise and bustle of worldly life is like the senseless shouts of the vulgar mob.

I was particularly interested in what you said about that strange Galilean teacher and healer, Jesus of Nazareth. Many of the sayings and teachings that you quoted bear much resemblance of those of the great Zeno. You know Zeno came from Citium in Cyprus, and it is said that he was a Phœnician by descent—that is, of the same race as your Jesus,—and undoubtedly the sources of his basic ideas were in the Orient. Yet Zeno's teaching was worked out, not amid the clouds of Asiatic mysticism, but in the clear sunlight of Hellenic rationalism, and so they are not muddled by the impractical absurdities of your Nazarene. Still I am glad, my Caius, that even such a man as he has turned your thoughts to serious things, and if you would take up the works of the great Zeno, and of his followers, Cleanthes and Chrysippus, and especially of the lucid Posidonius, you would soon reach the goal of perfect spiritual freedom and peace.

From what you write it seems to me that your preaching carpenter misses the main point. There is much that is noble in his sayings, but he is evidently without education or experience of the world. Had he left the narrow confines of his Galilee and traveled over our vast Empire, had he studied in the Portico and sat at the feet of our sages, he would have learned that the scheme of life he would inculcate is only for the few who can withdraw from the storms of this world and possess their souls in philosophic peace. In his proletarian ignorance he imagines that his

UNDER PONTIUS PILATE

Kingdom of Heaven is possible in this vile world of ours, that one can live and act in this den of wolves and yet retain his soul, instead of being torn in pieces if he does not become one of the stronger wolves. It is always just these impractical ideas that characterize the thinking of narrow and inexperienced minds.

If he were really a deep thinker, he would not waste his time going about an obscure country and through petty villages, preaching to ignorant peasants who can never understand such lofty doctrines; but rather would he have come to Athens, where for centuries all the great men of thought have gathered, and where his system, if partially false, would be corrected by keen criticism, and if true would be published over all the world with full authority. And if he had thoroughly understood the true essence of the life of virtue, he would not persist in healing people of their ills, but would rather teach them the loftier way of bearing trouble and suffering with noble silence and rising above them in godlike disdain.

As for these wonders you report, they may or

may not be exactly as you tell me. I do not doubt
your veracity, my Caius, for I myself have seen
marvels that at the time I could by no means understand, which afterward, for a small payment,
were explained and the trick made manifest.
Yet even if there be no trick in these things, they
do not prove anything except a somewhat unusual
power, which is also claimed for that Apollonius
of Tyana whom you mentioned, and for others
that I can not now recall.

It is not by legerdemain or even by actual
miracles that any system of true philosophy is
established. Not thus did the great Zeno pro-
mulgate the Stoic doctrine, not thus did Cleanthes and Aristippus and Chrysippus and the
divine Panetius establish the true tenets of our
noble philosophy. They proved their principles
by pure thought and in conformity with the laws
of Nature. The great law of life is that we should
act conformably to Nature. That a dead person
should stay dead is according to Nature; but to
raise the dead is certainly to act contrary to Nature, and so undermine the very foundations of
our being.

Besides, the violation of a natural law can not be accepted as adequate either to demonstrate or to refute a moral truth, since these things sustain no relation whatever to each other. It is as if one attempted to confute a hypothetical syllogism by blowing his nose. Such things are in no way related, and by such things the truth is confused. You must see, my Caius, that such expedients as the Galilean employs to spread his doctrine have the same moral value as the weeping children that the accused Athenian formerly introduced into the court of justice in order to overpower the reasoning faculties of the judges by exciting pity. It is to violate reason, outrage justice, and stifle truth, if one excites sympathy and gratitude, or prejudice and animosity. This can not show us the face of Truth. Heraclitus says, "the dry light is best," and surely it is only by the dry light of pure reason that the soul is illumined and the truth revealed.

What can an ignorant rabble of filthy Jews care for the truth, or what can an ill-trained peasant of Galilee teach us Romans, exercised in the highest Greek philosophy? I do not believe that any true system of philosophy can arise among that superstitious race. "I can not, like the Jew Apella, believe it," as you well said. To be sure some Jews in Alexandria, notably a certain Philo, are working at the old ideas of Plato, but, as it seems to me, they have merely succeeded in making that philosopher's obscure ideas more obscure. Certainly never has any illustrious or even capable disciple of that race appeared in the Portico or in the Academy. Some have come hither, of course, for what people is not represented in the schools of Athens? But these Jewish students have always failed to comprehend the divine truths taught by the founders and masters of our philosophy. Two or three years ago there was one of them here, a pleasant-looking fellow, of good breeding as Jews go,— the son of one of the Jewish Senators or Sanhedrists, I believe you call them,—of considerable wealth, and speaking Greek easily and fluently, who paid his talent to Apollonius, and began to attend his lectures on the *Pseudomenos* of Chrysippus. For three days he was all enthusiasm, the fourth day he forgot to bring his tablets, the fifth

day he went to sleep and snored like a Bœotian,
the sixth day he forfeited his fee for the lectures
and sailed back to Cæsarea, where I understand
he abuses the Stoics roundly, and buys and sells
female slaves openly in the market-place of his
native city.

And this Jesus is a Jew. I do not doubt
he is a remarkable personality, since he has
apparently affected you, my Caius, so deeply—
besides, has not the bewitching personality of the
Lady of Magdala had something to do with your
feelings also? But, my beloved Caius, beware of
personality. The power of personality affects the
emotions and the affections, and blinds the truth-
discerning eye of pure reason. Let pure thought
alone rule your mind, let pure thought alone guide
your footsteps; test every doctrine, even that of
the amiable Jesus, by the dry light of Heraclitus,
and then you can not err from the right way.

I feel sure, dearest Caius, if the fates give you
a few more years of life, that your noble nature
will completely tire of the disappointing chase
after pleasure, riches, and even fame; and that,
spurning insufficient teachers, you will, like me,

find peace and happiness in the calm of philosophic renunciation and the fortitude of noble poverty. For poverty is the strait path which leads to Virtue. When Virtue came down from Heaven and sought a dwelling among the children of men, the rich rejected her, the wicked threatened her, the powerful mocked her. She found no welcome save in the hut of Poverty. They have since dwelt together, having for a third companion, sweet Innocence, whom they took in as a forsaken foundling and nurtured. These are the true graces, Poverty, Virtue, and Innocence. Poverty and Virtue had no parents—they have always existed—and Innocence never knew her parentage—no one has claimed to have begotten her.

I am anxiously expecting your next letter, my Caius. There is nothing to write about here, as our life is so calm and uneventful and therefore so happy. Take good care of yourself in your exciting and dangerous surroundings. I shall be glad to clasp hands with you in Athens or anywhere. Farewell.

XII

Saul of Tarsus

XII

Caius Claudius Proculus in Cæsarea of Judea to Lucius Domitius Ahenobarbus in Athens sends greeting.

YOU may imagine, my beloved Lucius, how delighted I was when I came back here from Jerusalem to find your letter with its delicate aroma of the pure friendship that binds us together—the best thing I have known in my life. I am also delighted because you say that you have enjoyed these hastily indited narratives of my life in this strange land, and because you wish me to continue them as frequently as possible. You know well, my Lucius, that praise from you has always been most pleasing to me, from those early days when at school I used to wonder at your remarkable powers of learning as together we pored over the great poets, to the present time when the frivolous soldier, the shallow worldling, is compelled to revere the learned, subtle, and profound Stoic philosopher.

Your disquisition on the Galilean superstition and on the wonders worked by the new prophet is altogether worthy of your deep wisdom, and it brought you vividly before me with your calm, meditative eyes, and your measured and weighty words. Such wide learning and keen reasoning would have certainly removed all traces of the influence of the Nazarene's teaching had it been necessary; but as it is—since I wrote you from Tiberias—I have been so occupied with multifarious affairs that almost all thought of that strange teacher and wonder-worker has faded from my mind. Once in a while some saying of his will crop up, but the rush of business soon overwhelms it. You may rest easy, your friend Caius is in no danger of falling into the clutches of any Oriental superstition, even tho presented by a Jesus of Nazareth and exemplified by a Mary of Magdala; rather is he liable to degenerate into a mere machine for doing things. It takes, as you say, quiet and leisure to think thought of

182

any kind, and it takes considerable thinking to change a belief one has gradually grown into like my Epicureanism. When I again have a little time that I can call my own, I shall certainly follow your advice and read the works of your philosophers—and who knows but Caius Claudius may yet join Lucius Domitius in his colony of noble devotees of Poverty, Virtue, and Innocence? But now it is impossible.

This rush of business has also been the reason that so long a time elapsed between my last two letters. There has really been little to write about, as the details of military preparations would scarcely interest a philosopher. Herod's defeat has upset the quiet of the whole region. Not only, as I feared, have there been incursions of the wild Arabian horsemen across the southern border, but a large number of dissatisfied Israelites have joined together and have established themselves in the wilderness near the Dead Sea. They have been giving my good uncle, the procurator, all manner of trouble, as the band is so exceedingly desperate that none but the largest caravans with strong escorts dare to go by way of Jericho or Hebron. The leader of this gang is a certain Jesus Bar-Abbas, a pestilent fellow who was one of the ringleaders in the riot in the Temple that I told you about. He managed to kill several people in the affray, but had the fortune to escape unharmed out of the city into the wilderness; and now, taking advantage of the cloak of patriotism, is making his profit out of the general disturbance.

Pilate sent word of the matter to the propraetor Vitellius at Antioch; but Vitellius, who is not over fond of him, told him to go ahead and settle Bar-Abbas and his gang with his own forces, as the Syrian legions were fully occupied with keeping the Isaurians in order and in overawing the Parthians. For the same reason Vitellius, I understand, told Herod, who also applied to him for aid, to refer the matter to Caesar. So Herod has sailed for Rome, leaving the remnants of his forces to guard his frontiers with the aid of some troops of his half-brother Philip, the tetrarch of Gaulonitis and Iturea, which aid he has obtained by betrothing to him the fair and mischievous

SAUL OF TARSUS

Salome. Poor tetrarch! I do not envy him—for: bad mother, worse daughter.*

Well, about this matter of Bar-Abbas. Tho he has only a band of cut-throats behind him, he is making almost as much trouble as a regular campaign would, for fighting these sons of the desert is no light affair. The most elaborate preparations have to be made in the way of horses, arms, baggage, and supplies. You remember what happened to the great Crassus when he went into the desert against the Parthians. I know you will not care to hear the details of this business, but you will be interested in the news that Caius Claudius Proculus is to lead the expedition.

As this is my first independent command, you may believe I am expecting all sorts of glory, and am not neglecting a single thing that may make it a complete success. Syrus, that faithful rogue, is as enthusiastic as I am, and has really been of great use. He has managed to unearth from some of his subterranean resorts a couple of excellent guides who know the wilderness thoroughly —from former marauding expeditions I sup-

* Mater mala, filia deteriora.

185

pose—and the good fellow actually proposed to run up into Galilee, attach himself again to the Nazarene, and once more try to learn some of his magic, in order to assist in the campaign.

"If I only knew how Jesus made that bread!" he exclaimed, "I could be of some real service, and if I could manufacture wine from water our expedition would be a party of pleasure."

He was so filled with this idea that I had hard work to make him see that the time was too short to learn magic, even if there were any chance whatever of the Nazarene imparting such powers to any but his most trusted disciples, and that, besides, he was too useful to me just now for me to spare him.

In the last few days I have met a most interesting fellow, a young Jew named Saul of Tarsus, the strangest mixture you ever saw. He is a Roman citizen—by birth, too—yet a Pharisee of the straitest sort, and has been for some years studying the Jewish Law and Tradition in Jerusalem under the celebrated rabbi, Gamaliel. Saul's father in Tarsus had supplied my detachment with the light tents made of the Cilician

goat's hair, and Saul, who is on his way home—
to show his Rabbinical learning, I suppose—was
instructed by his father to close up the business
with me. He is a bright, vivacious Jew, of short
stature, with a long head and a prominent nose
set between a pair of kindly gray eyes. I was
attracted to him at once by his ease of manner and
fine courtesy, and then by the keen business sense
he displayed in securing everything that was due
him in the contract without in any way giving the
impression of being grasping or tricky.

He has a keen sense of wit, too, and, just as we
were finishing the first part of the affair, he let
fall an apt quotation from Menander. One
thing led to another, and to my surprise I found
my little Jew knew more about Greek literature
and philosophy than I did—at any rate he speaks
the language much more fluently. He knew a
great deal, too, about Philo, the Jewish philosopher of Alexandria whom you mentioned, and
seemed to have his writings at his tongue's end.
I am sure that, in spite of your prejudice against
the Jews, you would have been interested in what
he had to say about this philosopher who is now

attracting so much attention. It interested me
so much that before I knew it the dinner hour
arrived. I asked Saul to share my repast. In
an instant a complete change came over the vivacious Jew, and in a serious voice he said:

"Caius Claudius, you are a Roman, and you
are rightly proud of it, as your pride is caused by
the present greatness of your people, who now
rule the world, making all the nations pay them
tribute; and also you are descended from long
lines of great and noble men who have helped to
build up the greatness of your city. But I, tho
I enjoy the privileges of your citizenship, am
first and last a Hebrew, and I am proud of it.
And my pride is because I believe my people are
chosen from out all the earth by the one and
only God, to be his peculiar people and to keep
his Law, so that it may not perish from the earth.
I come from a long line of noble and wise men,
who have always punctiliously kept that Law,
even to its smallest details; and one of its require-
ments is that the true Israelite shall not eat with
the uncircumcised, lest what may be set before
him be, by our Law, unclean, and he thereby be

defiled. I know this seems absurd to you, a Roman; but I see you understand that I mean no discourtesy in refusing your honorable invitation."

He was so polite about it that I could not be offended; and when we met to settle the final payments, I again detained him to enjoy his conversation.

Our talk drifted to Herod and his late mishap. Saul's opinion was that the Herodian family has been the curse of his land, and, tho the great Herod had rebuilt the Temple and had extended the territories of Judea far beyond what they had ever been since the time of Solomon, yet it was his policy that had practically made the Romans masters of the country. Besides, he had persecuted and slaughtered the righteous men who kept the Law, and he himself had imitated the Gentiles in all his ways, so that his horrible death —he was eaten alive by lice, you may remember— had come upon him as a just retribution. And this son of his, Herod Antipas, was now suffering, because he, too, had followed in his father's footsteps and had slaughtered that holy man, John, called the Baptizer.

I told Saul then what I had heard and seen at Machærus. He was deeply interested, for he too had heard John preach at the fords of the Jordan.

"Certainly," he said, "John was a great teacher and a holy man of God. If he had not been slain, he would have become in time a rabban, as great as Hillel or Simeon; for he not only knew all the Law and the Traditions, but he lived up to them and knew how to draw the people to follow him. He would have done much to redeem Israel."

"Did you think he might be the Messiah?"

"Not at all. He fulfilled none of the conditions that are set forth so clearly in the prophets."

"Then he was a forerunner?"

"That idea was his one weakness. You know that all Jews believe in the coming of the Holy One of God, who shall set the chosen people at the head of the earth—sometime—in God's own good time—and John was especially firm in that belief. It was a great pity that, when he was in prison and could not see for himself, he should have been misled by reports of the miracles of Jesus of Nazareth and so declared him the Messiah."

"Then you do not believe in the miracles of the Nazarene?"

"I never saw them, and you know how things get exaggerated in the telling."

"My freedman, Syrus, swears that he himself saw Jesus cast out devils, feed five thousand people with five loaves, and walk on the Sea of Galilee as if it had been dry land."

"That may all be true; but it does not prove anything. There have been, and there will be false prophets working miracles by the power of Beelzebub to injure the chosen people of God and to lead them astray."

"How then can you tell a false prophet from a true one?"

"By his doctrine. If his teaching is in harmony with the Law and Tradition, then is he from God and a true prophet. But this fellow, Jesus, is constantly going against the Law. He never fasts and goes about feasting with publicans and sinners, he allows his disciples to pluck grain on the Sabbath, and to eat with unwashed hands, and he declares that many of our most cherished ceremonials and traditions are not only useless, but positively harmful. He attacks our saintliest men, calling them hypocrites and despoilers of widows' houses, and he would even destroy our Holy Temple and put an end to its services. And just before I left Jerusalem, I heard that he had declared himself the Son of God and said that he had come down from heaven, when everybody knows that he is of Nazareth, the son of a common carpenter. But that blasphemer draws thousands of those poor, ignorant Galileans after him, and even some of our most respectable Jews seem to have been affected. If only our Sanhedrim had yet the power of life and death, his career would soon be ended." As he proceeded the kindly light died out of his gray eyes, which were now flashing with passion, while his features hardened with inexorable hatred.

"Why do you think he ought to be slain? From what I heard of his teaching he is rather harmless than dangerous."

"Maybe to you,—Divide and conquer,* you remember. But to us the Nazarene is the sorest evil that has come upon us since Nebuchadnezzar

*Divide et impera.

192

destroyed Jerusalem, because he would overturn everything that makes God's people separate from the rest of the world. He would abolish our sacred Law and Ceremonials, which distinguish the Jew from the Gentile." Here Saul forgot my presence in the intensity of his emotion, and went on with his face turned toward Jerusalem. "But our hands are bound and will be bound till Shiloh come. We can not annihilate him as we ought to do; we can only pray: Let there be no hope to them who apostatize from the true religion; and let heretics, how many soever they be, all perish as in a moment. And let the kingdom of pride be speedily rooted out and broken in our days. Blessed art thou, O Lord our God, who destroyest the wicked and bringest down the proud." He finished the prayer in an ecstasy, then suddenly came to himself. "Pardon me, Caius Claudius," he said in his courteous tone. "But my regard for the honor of the God of Israel sometimes overcomes my sense of what is fitting. I shall instantly forget that I am an Israelite and only remember that I am a Roman citizen."

UNDER PONTIUS PILATE

If Saul expresses the feeling of the Pharisees, I fear that the road of the gentle Nazarene will be a hard one. And yet there is something grand and impressive in this devotion of a whole race to the loftiest ideal of Divinity, even if it does lead to an exasperating exclusiveness which manifests itself in foolish formalities.

Saul sailed yesterday for Tarsus, and to-morrow we sail for Gaza. Our plan is to get between Bar-Abbas and the Arabian desert and run him down in the wilderness of Judea. Consequently it may be some time before I can send a letter to you. But write to me, my Lucius, just the same. Everything that comes for me to Cæsarea will be forwarded to Jericho, where I shall get it when I come up from the south after finishing Bar-Abbas. One thing bothers me a little, however; I do not feel as well as I should; I can not tell exactly what is the matter with me, and perhaps it will wear off in the excitement of the expedition. Military movements always bring out the best that is in me. But wish for my health as I do for yours, my Lucius. Farewell.

Part II

THE SON OF GOD

XIII

The Gates of Death

XIII

Caius Claudius Proculus in Jericho of Judea to Lucius Domitius Ahenobarbus in Athens sends greeting.

YOUR dear letters, my Lucius, which I found awaiting me when I arrived here, have aroused me somewhat from my dull misery and have inspired me to dictate this reply by the hand of the faithful Syrus. In spite of the fearful disease which is slowly finishing me, the devoted fellow has never left my side, since it progressed far enough to render me partially helpless. The truth is that I have somehow contracted this horrible leprosy, which is so prevalent in the hot and dry lands of the East. The first symptoms I think began to show themselves just before I left Cæsarea last August, but I was so taken up with the expedition against Bar-Abbas, that I paid little or no attention to it until the campaign was about over, and then it had a complete hold on me. Now I am almost helpless. No physician can do anything except prolong my agony, for the few cases where the patient has recovered seem to have cured themselves. But in my case the best physician here gives no hope; he can only promise to make my demise as little painful as possible. So you see:

"Relentless Death, that formerly gloomed from afar,
    Has suddenly quickened his pace and beckons me hence." *

I wish it would hurry faster, for my present condition is dull enough. There might have been some excitement in making my exit during one of the fierce skirmishes Bar-Abbas and I had in the wilderness among the wintry hills, and I might have had the chance of finding out whether it is as Horace says:

    "A grateful and a glorious deed
        To perish for our country's need." †

But why should I complain? Tho I have

* Semotique prius tarda necessitas
        Leti corripuit gradum.—*Horace*.
† Dulce et decorum est pro patria mori.

not seen many years, I have lived so thoroughly there does not seem much that I have not experienced, except, of course, the joys and woes of sovereignty, which are out of my reach. All my old delights were beginning to pall on me, and the glory and honor of my independent command were not what I had expected. I have no desire for further promotion when I think of the cares and anxieties of my good uncle, between the irritable Jews beneath and the gross Vitellius above, with the suspicious and unspeakable Tiberius in the distance. Life might have been worth living in the old days when Romans were free men and a man's great deeds were always for his country and his gods, when brave and noble men were crowned in triumph amid the plaudits of a free people; but when one thinks that all his efforts in the front of battle or in the prætorium serve merely to increase the tribute from downtrodden peoples—tribute that only enlarges the amount of provender of such gormandizing swine as Vitellius, or pays for the unmentionable orgies of Capreæ—why, it really makes no difference whether Caius Claudius Proculus pass away pierced by a hostile javelin or consumed by an Oriental disease—except that the former way is the more agreeable. You may think this is dangerous talk to dictate to even such a faithful soul as Syrus; but I shall be nothing when this reaches you, and you can destroy the dangerous words as soon as you have read them.

I am now in my tent outside of the walls of Jericho. Of course, as a Roman commander, I might have quartered myself in the town, in spite of the Jewish law that such bits of corruption as I am must keep out of walled cities; but I am too far gone to go through with the trouble such a step would involve, or to want to feel the hatred and disgust I should arouse. In fact, I think I can understand how the people must feel, for at present I am an object of utter abhorrence to myself. And besides, in this beautiful spring weather, it is far more comfortable in my spacious tent in the meadows than in some narrow room within those stifling walls.

My sole idea is to get to Jerusalem to put my affairs into good condition, so that none of my hand. When the good Syrus had written the word "Farewell," he could no longer contain himself, but burst into tears and fled from the tent. He has never given up hope of my recovery, and this morning he told me that he had heard of the Nazarene's being lately in Jericho, and that he was now in Peræa, not far from here. He begged me to go to him and be healed, and added that he had seen worse cases than mine healed at Capernaum. But what is the good of my being jostled about over the wilds of Peræa running after an inspired carpenter? I think that faith in him was the condition of every cure I saw or heard of, but I do not possess any faith, nor have I energy enough to manufacture it for the occasion. Anyhow, it is not worth while. I do not care enough about living, and really think it best that I should be he

> "Who now shall travel o'er that shadowy road,
> Whence no one is permitted to return." *

So, my best-beloved friend, "half of my soul," †
I, on the threshold of death, salute you. And

* Qui nunc it per iter tenebricosum
 Illuc, unde negant redire quemquam.—*Catullus.*
† Animæ dimidium meæ.—*Horace.*

family will lose anything, and then—I have my good sword, and I have not forgotten "Cato's noble death," *

"Nor is death hard to me who am about to put away griefs by death." †

And my well-beloved Lucius, as

"Death is the last line of all things," ‡

I might as well tell you briefly of my expedition, and so conclude the story of my life in Judea—which I promised you.

As we came into the wilderness of Judea from the south, we drove Bar-Abbas and his band northward. Pilate had posted a strong detachment near Jericho, which threw him back on my hands and forced him to make a desperate effort to break through my line. It was a superb fight, and I had a lively time of it for quite a while, for not only were his followers filled with the courage of despair, but Bar-Abbas himself has considerable military knowledge, and a keen eye for his enemy's weak points. At one time I feared I had lost him, but in the end our Roman

* Catonis nobile letum.—*Horace.*
† Nec mihi mors gravis est posituro morte dolores.—*Virgil.*
‡ Mors ultima linea rerum est.—*Lucretius.*

arms and discipline prevailed, and, after the greater part of his force had been slain, the rest retreated into the mountains.

From that time on it was a long but often exciting man-hunt, which lasted for months, clear through the winter. Since I was obliged to divide my force into small bodies, any one who got separated from his companions was lost, and a couple of times a whole detachment fell into an ambush and was cut off to a man. No mercy was asked or shown on either side. I must give due credit to Syrus and his subterranean friends for their admirable service as guides; we never should have succeeded had it not been for their aid, by which we finally ran down Bar-Abbas and the last remnant of his band in a cave in the mountains.

The fight was the most desperate encounter I have ever seen, for the robbers realized that

"The only safety to them left
Was that they were of hope bereft." *

As I had not my full strength on account of the leprosy, Bar-Abbas beat me down, and would have happily finished me, but unfortunately

* Una salus victis nullam sperare salutem.—*Virgil*.

202

Longinus, my favorite centurion, best and kept off the gigantic fellow, while Syr me out of the mess and set me on my fe Well, in the end, after losing quite a n our men, we slew them all except the and two of his lieutenants—Dysmas and as brave a trio of desperadoes as you e They are to decorate a hill near Jerusa tooned on crosses, so that the rest of may be encouraged in their obedience.

I had intended entering Jerusalem captives and trophies; but now I feel tha rest here a few days, and so shall send the ahead with the most of my force under tenant. This letter will go with them reach you, my beloved friend, when I nothing—nowhere—

"For earthly suns may set and rise again,
But when the sun of life sets,—then, ah! t
Eternal sleep envelops gods and men." *
Farewell.

. . . .

I write these concluding lines with

* Soles occidere et redire possunt
Nobis, cum semel occidit brevis lux,
Nox est perpetua una dormienda.—*Catul*

203

THE GATES OF DEATH

do you, when you read this, pour out a libation
in memory of me — since, to twist Horace's
lines,

> "You may not with your tears bedew
> The face your gentle friendship knew." *

Again, farewell.

> * Calentem
> Non sparges lacrima favillam
> Levis amici.—*Horace.*

XIV
Faith, Hope, and Love

XIV

Faith, Hope, and Love

XIV

At Bethany

WELL, my beloved Lucius, after having read all the lugubrious poetry which filled my last letter—you would scarcely imagine I had such a memory—and, after having poured a libation in memory of me, this epistle will surely astonish you—unless perhaps it overtake the other on the way. And, what is more astonishing, not only am I still living, but I am willing, nay even determined to live—if I can. All my desire for "Cato's noble death" has vanished, and— just imagine!—I am even beginning to think that Cato's death was not so noble after all, in spite of what philosophers and poets have written about it. Ovid says truly

"He is a coward who longs for death," *

for the fear of death often is by no means as great as the fear of life under adverse fates. Which is

* Timidi est optare necem.

the nobler—to leave this life when it displeases us, or, with an unconquerable spirit, to bear patiently whatever ills the gods may send us? You, as a good Stoic, know it is well

"To keep a calm mind amid adverse fates." *

I see the smile come over your face when you read this, and I hear your laugh when you read that the cause of this sudden change in spirit is nothing less than Mary of Magdala. "Ah!" you say, "it is the old chain, the old insanity; some of Mary's devils have surely established a colony in the brain of Caius Claudius." But you are wrong; it is not the old chain of servitude; it is a new life of freedom that Mary is opening unto me.—I see again your incredulous smile— but you must take my word for it—it is the truth. I feel no longer any of my old desire for Mary the hetaira—it is hard for me now to imagine how it ever could exist; instead, there is a pure and noble feeling of honor, far beyond that paid to the memory of the chaste Lucretia; for Mary has risen out of the seething whirlpool of passion

* Æquam . . . rebus in arduis
Servare mentem.

and has ascended the calm, white heights of
purity. No one can be near her without feeling
it, and by this lofty purity she is uplifting my
soiled soul from the mire wherein it wallowed,
and is revealing to it the highest things. I used
to say "Dust and a shade are we," * but now I
see we must be something more than this, and
I am beginning, under Mary's guidance, to find
gleams of that bright something in the turbid
depths of my own being. As Ovid says:

"There is a god within us and the fellowship of heaven;
To us from those celestial seats the breath of life is given." †

And I am even ready to say in my disease as he
did in his lonely exile:

"That I am still alive, is the free gift of God." ‡

You wonder probably how this remarkable
thing happened to your light-headed friend, who
had lived so long contented with a shallow Epicureanism. Well, the faithful Syrus was respon-
sible for the whole matter. I wrote you, I believe,
how he had urged me to go to the Nazarene and

*Pulvis et umbra sumus.—*Horace.*
†Est deus in nobis et commercia Cœli,
Sedibus ætheriis spiritus ille venit.
‡Id quoque quod vivam, munus habere dei.

be healed.   But I had noticed that these wonderful events always occur among credulous people, and never happen to those of skeptical mind. A certain amount of faith on the part of the patient seems absolutely necessary, and I had heard the Master at Capernaum say to several that their faith had healed them.   I was certain I did not, and could not, have that faith, and so, as I wrote you, I thought it would be a useless agony to be jostled about the rough roads of the Jordan valley, trying to catch a wandering rabbi, who probably could not help me even if I found him.

But Syrus was persistent.   He offered himself to hunt up the Nazarene and bring him to me—being absolutely confident in his powers of persuasion, and they are undoubtedly great; but I could not allow him to beg anything from Jesus, after having abandoned him on account of his doctrine.   At last, in order to stop his well-meant importunities, I ordered Syrus to move me to Jerusalem—a long day's journey.

We expected to reach the city just before the time for closing the gates, and so pushed on as rapidly as I could bear. As we were passing through the village of Bethany, a couple of miles from the city, I saw in front of one of the best houses a woman, whose attitude seemed familiar, looking off toward the east; but as we approached the house she went inside. When we were just opposite the doorway, Syrus, who was riding beside my litter, wavered in his saddle and sank to the ground as if about to swoon away. My slaves called for help, and out of the house came three women, accompanied by some servants, to bring aid. Imagine my surprise when I recognized Mary of Magdala, her sister Martha, and Susanna.

I pulled the curtains of my litter together, so that they should not see me in my frightful state, and said I would remain outside while they attended to my man. It was over two hours before the rascal would speak, and then as it was far past the time for closing the gates, we were obliged to stay over night in Bethany

Syrus told Mary, what she had suspected before, that I was outside, and the two came out together and absolutely forced me to enter the house, in

spite of my objections on account of my leprosy.
I will confess, my Lucius, that a little of my old
vanity came in here. However, Mary said that she
had learned much from the Master about cleanness
and uncleanness, and that no work of kindness
or mercy could ever defile a house or a human
being. Besides, the strict rules that are applied
to Jewish lepers were not generally enforced
against strangers and sojourners. And then,
with the air of one accustomed to command, she
ordered my slaves to bear the litter inside.

It was a sharp trick of Syrus; and he has con-
fessed it. As soon as he had recognized Mary
standing at the doorway, he, knowing well how
much I thought of her, determined to have her
influence added to his, and so here I am. Four
days have passed, and I am likely to stay on in-
definitely, at least until after the Passover. Mary
has persuaded me to live.

She has taken the care of my repulsive person
upon herself, assisted only by the indefatigable
Syrus and the dear little Susanna. It is quite
interesting to see how Syrus, by his boundless
willingness and never-failing good humor, has

won the affection of the whole household. Susanna seems especially taken with him. I constantly hear her merry laugh when they are together, and she can hardly look at him without a friendly smile lighting up her pretty face. But Mary's patience and loving-kindness are wonderful. She bathes me, cares for my couch, brings me cooling drinks, prepares my food with her own hands, and spends hours entertaining me, not only without the slightest repugnance, but as if it were a great privilege. I never saw anything like it before. Martha, who owns the house and farm, is continually busy, looking after its direction, but every now and then she finds a little time to sit down and listen to Mary's beautiful stories of the Master, which I must confess I find more and more interesting each day.

The Master is expected to come here a little before the Passover, to stay through the feast, and both sisters insist that I must await his coming and be healed. When I spoke about my not having faith, Mary replied:

"There is no doubt, Caius, that faith is a great aid. The Master himself said that my faith had saved me.. But Peter told me that he had healed the daughter of a Syro-Phœnician woman, and also the slave of a Roman centurion, without going near them, on account of the faith of the mother and the master. Perhaps he only requires faith in Israelites or in some one who cares, and, Caius, he himself has said that I have faith. And so I do not doubt."

"But, Mary, what is this faith of yours? What is it that you believe?"

"That there is one God, who has made heaven and earth, that he is our Father, and that Jesus is his beloved son, the Christ, whom he has sent to redeem the world."

Lucius, it is impossible to imagine anything more beautiful than her face as she uttered these words. I gazed at her in dumb adoration.

"I wish I had your faith, Mary," I murmured at last.

"You will have it, Caius, some time. It will come to you when you least expect it, like a thief in the night, and then you will not only be healed in your body, but your soul will have eternal life."

FAITH, HOPE, AND LOVE

"How can you prove that you have eternal life?"

"Why should I prove it? I know it. Do I not know that I breathe? Even so I know that the breath of eternal life is in my soul. You know what I was before the Master saved me. Did you ever come up out of a deep dark cave into the brilliant light of midday?—There is no God but God, and Jesus is his Christ."

When I told her that I did not care for life, that I was sick of all my old pleasures and of my dreams of glory, and that I did not think this world had anything to offer that would make life worth living, she said:

"You are right about *this* world; it has nothing to make life worth living. So I found it, and so you now find it. But the life eternal! Ah, that is so different! it is a joy to live."

"How do you live the life eternal, Mary?"

"You have lived it."

"I?"

"Yes, I know of one time, and I do not doubt that there are many others. Have you ever regretted what you did for Susanna?"

"Why should I? It was nothing."

"Does it still please you when you think of her pure and happy life here?"

"Naturally."

"Have any of your other pleasures lasted like this?"

"I see, Mary, you want me to live a life like yours."

"No, Caius, I want you to live your own life—but at its highest. I want you to live your eternal life." And then she went on to tell me how faith brought about this eternal life, and of its peace and happiness. For these last, I need no other evidence but her blessed face. And so she has persuaded me to try to get this faith, or at any rate to abide here until the Master comes.

They have placed my couch in the central court by the fountain, and have spread an awning over it, so I am quite comfortable. I feel glad that I am, as it were, in the midst of their beautiful life, and am not thrust away in some chamber, no matter how elegant it might be.

This afternoon Lazarus came out from Jerusalem, to attend to some business of his sisters, and Martha found time to sit down for a while and talk. The conversation soon turned to the Master. Martha and Lazarus had some dispute about one of his sayings, but finally settled it by referring to Mary, whose wording proved to be somewhat different from either of theirs. Yet both seemed perfectly satisfied to accept her version. When Mary had gone out for an instant, I asked the reason of this.

"Why," answered Martha, "Mary is the only one of us who really understands the Master, and she never forgets a syllable. When he was with us at the Feast of Tabernacles, last autumn, we erected a beautiful booth for him, right here where your couch is, and Mary established herself at his feet and did nothing but listen to his words. Now, as this was his first visit to us, I felt we should do him all honor, and I turned the house upside down to have everything the very best possible. As you may imagine, I was worried about many things, but, tho Mary had worked hard enough before, she had not, since the Master came, stirred from her place at his feet. It put me just a little out of temper to think of her idling, while I was doing everything for the guest, who had been invited mainly on her account. So, the more I hurried about, the warmer I became, and the hotter my temper. Finally I stopped before the booth and said:

"'Master, does it not trouble you to see my sister leaving me alone to minister unto you? Tell her to come and help me.'

"But he replied with a smile: 'Martha, Martha, you are anxious and disturbed about many things. But one thing is needful. Mary has chosen the better part which shall not be taken away from her.'

"And then it flashed upon me how stupid I had been. We were going to have the Master with us for a short time only, and we knew that he was satisfied with the simplest things, and here was I wasting the precious moments of his visit, bustling about, to see that the dinner should be especially fine. And he had said that the life was more than meat and the body than raiment. Truly Mary had chosen the better part, and I, abashed, asked if I might sit beside her and listen too. But I do not remember his words as she does. What do you suppose is the reason, Lazarus?"

CHRIST WITH MARY AND MARTHA, from the painting by H. Siemiradzki

"Mary established herself at his feet and did nothing but listen to his words."

FAITH, HOPE, AND LOVE

"Perhaps it is because of the great love Mary bears him," he replied.

Lucius, do not laugh—I am already convinced that, as Mary says, the greatest thing in the world is Love. Love, simple, pure, and undefiled— Love eternal. Farewell.

XV
Death

WHEN BOSTON BRAVE

XV

At Bethany

A TERRIBLE thing has happened to this dear household, Lucius. The day after Larazus's arrival, he was taken suddenly with a malignant fever. Martha immediately sent to the city for a physician, and Mary despatched one of her servants to Bethabara—where she had news that the Master was staying—to tell him that Lazarus was ill. But before the second day was ended, the young man had suddenly, without warning, as it were, passed away.

I tried to comfort the bereaved sisters, but my poor efforts were not of much avail, and, knowing what a great trouble, and perhaps grievous hindrance, I and my disease would be when the friends and relations would come for the funeral, I proposed that, as I was so much better, and even able to move about a little, I should go on to

Jerusalem. But Mary would not allow it. Even in her deep grief she still thought of me, and insisted that I must await the Master, who would soon be here. So the most that I could get her to agree to was that I should pitch my tent at the border of the village on a little eminence above the road, and that Syrus and Susanna should minister to my wants from the house.

I left just before the friends and the mourners arrived, and now I can hear the sounds of weeping and wailing coming from the house whence the funeral is soon to take place; for with the Jews the interment must be within a day of the demise. The body is to be laid in the family tomb, which is hollowed out of the hillside near by. From my tent I can see it plainly, as well as the preparations for the burial.

I feel a deep sense of personal loss, my Lucius, for tho I had seen but little of Lazarus, yet there was something lovable about him that attracted me irresistibly. His was a nature of great refinement—and the refinement of these Orientals is an exquisite thing—and with this was a youthful frankness that was extremely engaging. Tho

he, like his sisters, had believed in the Master,
and, as Mary had told me, had been greatly
beloved by him, yet he had never joined himself
to the body of disciples that follow the Master's
footsteps, nor had he ceased to fulfil all the Jewish
observances as a good Pharisee. So he was not
involved in the hatred of the Master that Syrus
tells me has been showing itself in Jerusalem
during the past few months, and which he thinks
has caused the Master to withdraw out of the
province into Peræa. So the hosts of friends that
the lovable young fellow had made in Jerusalem,
and the many members of his prominent family,
have all thronged out here to honor his memory
and to condole with his sisters.

Poor Mary! She has been kept close within
doors, but even in her grief she has not forgotten
me, but has sent an encouraging message by
Susanna, bidding me to hope and to trust, for
my deliverance is near. And as for her, tho she
can not understand her own bereavement, she
still trusts in the Lord, who does all things well.
This remembrance is exceedingly sweet to me.
Mary can well say with Dido:

UNDER PONTIUS PILATE

"I learn, since grief hath touched my heart,
Pity to feel and aid impart."*

I am sitting oustide my tent, watching the wide
stretch of desert way leading to Jericho. The
Master might, by making great haste, reach
here to-night—too late. But is it too late?
Stories are told of his raising the dead in Galilee.
Still, one case, a little girl, had died but an hour
before his arrival, and the other, a young man,
I believe was only a few hours dead. Those may
have only seemed dead—such cases are not un-
known—but Lazarus's death from that malignant
disease is only too certain. What a pity the
Master could not have come sooner!

Just now the messenger sent by Mary arrived,
exhausted by the speed he had made. Syrus
intercepted him and asked the news. The Master had said that this sickness was not unto death,
but for the glory of God, so that the Son of God
might be glorified by it. This certainly does not
show omniscience. Why could he not have
healed Lazarus as he did the servant of the centurion and the daughter of the Syro-Phœnician
woman that Mary told me about? I can not

*Non ignara mali, miseris succurrere disco.—*Virgil.*

understand, and I have not the faith of Mary. It seems that, if ever there were a fit place for a miracle, it was here. But I fear the Master's powers are not so great as they are thought to be. I only wish that, for Mary's sake, if for no other reason, he had sent his word of power to that poor, sick youth before it was too late. But his ways are past finding out. I can not see——

A remarkable thing has just occurred. While I was writing, Syrus came up, and, begging pardon for interrupting me, said that he had a request to make.

"Any request of yours, my faithful fellow, is granted before you ask it. What may it be?"

"Master," he said, "I am but a clumsy servitor. What you need most is a woman's care."

"But I have that now. Susanna is almost equal to Mary."

"No one knows that better than I, master. But we can not always abide in Bethany, and, tho the Master will surely heal you of your present infirmity, yet other ills may happen to you. I have seen only too plainly, since we have been here, how totally inadequate was my care of you.

229

Think how much better you have become since you have had the Lady of Magdala and Susanna to attend you."

"That is perfectly true—but what under heaven are you driving at, Syrus? What *is* your request?"

"It is this. You see you may need the care of a woman—not of a slave, of a hireling—but of a woman who will serve you from gratitude, from love. And that is what I can procure for you, if you will grant my request."

"You talk in enigmas, Syrus. Come to the point," I interrupted, somewhat impatiently.

"Well, master, I want you—after the funeral, of course, and when the mourners have departed— to ask the Lady of Magdala to give her consent to my wedding her freedwoman, Susanna——"

"Syrus!" I could not find words to express my amazement.

"You will ask her, will you not, master?—in your own good time, of course."

"But, Syrus, Susanna will never leave Mary," I managed to say at last.

"Susanna and I have talked it over. She can

never forget what you have done for her, and she wishes to make some small return. And you know how it is with me. Our cases are much alike. Susanna says she will never leave her mistress without her consent; but that, otherwise, she is not only willing but anxious to serve you."

"Are you sure," I asked, laughing, "that the desire of serving me is the sole motive that inspires you two?"

"Well, master," began Syrus—and then he broke into one of his irresistible smiles—"I will admit that she is truly a fair and goodly maiden——"

"And also that her suitor is an exceedingly clever and engaging personage."

"But really, master, you know well that it delights us both to serve you, and as husband and wife we could do many things for you that would otherwise be impossible."

"I know it, Syrus, and I fully appreciate your devotion, and Susanna's, too. I know I do not deserve it, for what I did for you two was merely to gratify a passing whim——"

"It was no whim, master, but the boundless generosity of your noble nature——"

231

UNDER PONTIUS PILATE

"That will do, Syrus, you quite spoil me. I suppose that, since I have given my word, I must fulfil your request, and I do not doubt that Mary will give her consent, and, for that matter, look upon your schemes as you do."

The fellow fell at my feet, to show his gratitude. And now I can hear the subdued but joyous chatter of the two from the tent. How strange, my Lucius, is the irresistible force of Nature, which for mysterious purposes drives living beings together! O wondrous power of Venus! You remember Lucretius says:

"Venus benign! 'Tis by thy gentle grace
    The fruitful earth and the sail-bearing sea
With life are teeming. From the soft embrace,
    Wherein begins thy wondrous mystery,
    All living creatures quicken to their birth,
By thee spring into life, exult, and fill the earth." *

And now here, in this little corner of the earth, in the midst of loathsome disease, grim death, and heartrending sorrow, Venus still, in the most

*Alma Venus, cœli subter labentia signa
    Quæ mare navigerum, quæ terras frugiferentes
    Concelebras; per te quoniam genus omne animantum
    Concipitur, visitque exortum lumina solis.

232

DEATH

unforeseen ways, does her eternal work. I, too,
must give thanks to her.

"Mother of the Roman race! delight of gods and men!" *

for I see well that my own future comfort will be
greatly increased by this latest manifestation of
her divine power. I wonder what effect Susanna's
dainty nature will have on Syrus's grosser clay.

The funeral has just passed by—the bier
accompanied by the family and followed by the
hired mourners. Tho the wailing and the howling of the hirelings were a sore trial to my ears, I
dragged myself after them at a little distance,
and stood on a small eminence hard by the tomb
to show my respect for the departed youth. I
hope Mary saw me. I wrote a few words of con-
dolence in Greek and sent them to her by Susanna.
Now

"Dark night enfolds me in her hollow shades," . . .
and

"With night my cares return." †

It is very dark.

*Æneadum genetrix, hominum divomque voluptas!
—*Lucretius.*

†Nox atra cava circumvolat umbra . . .
Sub noctem cura recursat.—*Virgil.*

233

XVI
Resurrection

XVI

At Bethany

MY beloved Lucius, I shall try to tell you the marvelous story in regular order, without comment, and do you make out of it what you can.

The days passed slowly after the burial of Lazarus—dark, dreary days. When the stone had been rolled before the door of the tomb, most of the crowd went back to Jerusalem, but quite a number of friends and relatives remained, according to the Jewish custom, to condole with the sisters. I know Mary would have preferred to be alone, but she has endured all calmly and patiently.

The second day she stole away from the house to the tomb to weep there alone. On her way back, she stopped to say an encouraging word to me.

"But, Mary," I asked, "why has the Master not yet come? Could he have heard of Lazarus's death and turned back?"

"No, no. There is some good reason for his delay. But he will come."

"What faith you have, Mary! Do you ever doubt?"

"I hope not, Caius. I always pray for the faith of Job, who said, 'Tho he slay me, yet will I trust in him.' I believe that Jesus knows the will of his Father in Heaven and does it. This sorrow of ours must be for some perfect reason. I can not understand it; but what would become of me if I should cease to believe on him!"

"O you wonderful woman!" I exclaimed.

"God bless you, Caius, and bring you all health and happiness!" And she disappeared.

The fourth day after the burial, as I was sitting in front of my tent, looking down the Jericho road, which makes a steep descent just outside the village, I saw a small party coming up the hill, at a deliberate gait. As they drew nearer, I could make out the Master, accompanied by five of his disciples. I recognized John and

RESURRECTION

Peter and Judas, but the others I had not seen
before. I called Syrus and sent him to tell the
sisters the news. In a little while he returned
with Martha, who met the Master on the road,
just below where I was sitting.

"Master," I heard her say, "had you been
here my brother had not died. And even now
I know that whatever you ask of God, God will
give it to you."

"Your brother will rise again," the Master
said softly.

"Yes, I know he will rise again in the resurrection at the last day."

"I am the resurrection and the life," said Jesus.
"He that believes on me, tho he die, yet shall he
live; and whoever lives and believes on me, shall
never die. Do you believe this, Martha?"

"Yes, Master," she replied, "I have believed
that you are the Christ, the Son of God who
should come into the world. But let me call my
sister."

"Go. But call her secretly."

When Martha had gone, the Master glanced
up and saw me, where I stood above him.

"Who are you?" he asked.

"The leper, Caius Claudius."

"Who came with Mary of Magdala to hear me near Capernaum, and then rode away because you were afraid."

"I was afraid that I might believe in your teachings," I replied, astonished at his knowing my thoughts on that occasion.

"Come down, Caius Claudius."

Without hesitation I clambered down—wondering neither at the alacrity of my obedience nor at the ease of my descent.

When I stood before him, he laid his hand on my shoulder, and, gazing into my eyes with a look that penetrated into the innermost depths of my being, he asked:

"Are you afraid yet, or are you willing to believe?"

"I believe."

"What do you believe?"

"That you can heal me if you will."

"So be it, Caius Claudius."

Just then I saw Mary hastening down the road, the red gold of her disheveled hair floating about her face. She fell at the Master's feet, crying like her sister:

"Had you been here my brother had not died."

Behind her came Martha and many of the friends; and they stood near weeping. Then, with a troubled expression on his face, the Master asked:

"Where have you laid him?"

"Come and see."

The Master wept. And I heard some one say, "See how he loved him!" But one who stood just below me murmured, "Could not this man, who opened the eyes of the blind man, have kept his friend from death?"

Martha led the way to the tomb. I followed, at a little distance behind the crowd. When they came before the grave, Jesus said:

"Take away the stone."

"Master," interrupted Martha, "by this time he is corrupted, for he has been dead four days."

"Did I not say to you," Jesus answered, "that if you believed, you would see the glory of God?" So they rolled away the stone, and Jesus, lifting up his eyes, said: "Father, I thank thee that thou heardest me. And I knew that thou hearest me always; but because of the multitude which stand around I said it, so that they may believe that thou didst send me." And then, turning toward the tomb, he cried with a loud voice, "Lazarus, come forth."

And the dead man came forth, bound hand and foot in his grave clothes. Then, as he stood there in the bright light, trembling, Jesus said:

"Loose him and let him go."

There, Lucius, those are the facts—no logic, no dialectic, can controvert what I saw with my own eyes and heard with my own ears. And I believe that the Master is—what I can not say yet. But one thing I do know. He is more than man.—And he may be the Son of God.

But I see that I have forgotten to give the conclusion of another incident, which is of considerable importance—at least to me. Look back at the words of the Master to me just before Mary ran to meet him. I must say that I was so absorbed in what followed that I temporarily forgot what those words were. And, as the joyous throng, with Jesus in their midst, came up the

THE RAISING OF LAZARUS, from the painting by Rubens

"And the dead man came forth. . . . Then as he stood there in the bright light, trembling, Jesus said, 'Loose him, and let him go.'"

THE RAPE OF LUCRETIA. By the Master of Modena.

road to the house, I turned to go back into my tent.   But the Master called to me:

"Come with us, Caius Claudius."

"I can not," I replied, "I am unclean."

All turned and looked at me, and Mary cried out:

"Caius, Caius, you are healed!"

I stood stock still, in dumb amazement, while Syrus ran into the tent and, bringing out a mirror, held it before me.   Lucius—this is the truth— my flesh was as soft and clean as that of a little child.   I felt the full tide of life and health coursing through my veins.   And I fell at the feet of the Master.

XVII

The Kingdom of Heaven

XVII

At Jerusalem

HERE I am, my Lucius, after many months, back in my old quarters in the Antonia Tower, which overlooks the Temple. I have a fine view of the Mount of Olives, behind which lies Bethany, the scene of the greatest marvel the world has ever known.

All through the evening after the raising of Lazarus, we sat in the court of Martha's house, talking mostly about the great event. All of us, except the Master, were very curious to know if Lazarus could tell us anything of that other world which he had visited. He was perfectly frank and said:

"Have you not fallen asleep in the evening, and then in the morning awakened with the consciousness of having had some wondrous dream, but with no other recollection expect that the dream was beyond all comparison mar-

247

velous? So it is with me. I fell asleep—you tell me—four days ago. The Master's voice roused me to-day. There was something wonderful in the interim. This is all I can tell you—except that I am glad to be here with you dear ones again."

When he concluded, there was silence, for we all wanted to hear what the Master would say. But he sat smiling as if waiting for one of us to speak. Lucius, there is something in that man's face that impresses you more and more, the oftener you look upon it. As he sat there with that questioning smile, it was the face of a simple, loving man, who drew your heart to him as irresistibly as an affectionate child, and for the same reason; but when he stood before the tomb and cried, "Lazarus, come forth," his face was as the face of a God; and between these two extremes runs an infinity of expression which covers the whole range of the human and even the superhuman. As none of us spoke, the Master turned to me and asked:

"Caius Claudius, what do you think of Lazarus' words?"

THE KINGDOM OF HEAVEN

"Master," I replied, "I formerly believed that our life ended with our breath; but now, since Lazarus has returned, I know that we are eternal. My motto was, as we Romans say, *Carpe diem*, or, as others have it, 'Eat, drink, and be merry, for to-morrow we die.' But now I know we should live not so much for this life here on earth, as for the life to come,—in heaven. And therefore, Master, teach us somewhat of that life; for in that life, I suppose, we shall find the Kingdom which you proclaim."

"No, Caius Claudius, you will not have to wait for that life to behold the Kingdom; for the Kingdom of Heaven is within you, here and now, and, just as you open your eyes in the morning and behold the light of the sun, so you only need to open the eyes of your soul to behold the Kingdom of Heaven in all its glory."

And then, my Lucius, the Master went on to unfold his teaching of the spiritual kingdom which he says he is sent to bring among us. As he spoke I knew he was right—that all our earthly ideals and philosophies—even your noble Stoicism, my Lucius—are either all wrong or miss the one thing needful—the faith that God, the maker of all things, is not something distinct and separate and far removed from us; but that he is bound up in us, and we in him, the noble and the slave, the good and the evil—all brothers, sons of the eternal Father. Our old desires of material greatness, wealth, and power at each other's expense, that old saying, "Man devours man," are the errors which have caused our sin and misery; and if we, like the Master, love instead of hate, cherish instead of despise, aid instead of contend with our brother men, then all our transitory troubles will pass away, and infinite happiness and eternal peace will come to us.

But this time, after the Master had finished speaking, there were no doubts to creep into my mind, as before at Capernaum. I have written down all that he said, for it is engraved deep within my heart. I shall not, however, send it to you—at least not now—for I know you would receive it with calm, philosophical contempt. The Master said that his Kingdom had been concealed from the wise and revealed unto babes—that we must be born again to enter into it. I believe that I went through the pangs of death in my leprosy, and that I was born again under the Master's healing touch; for my old self seems as tho it were dead, and the present Caius Claudius is as simple and as happy as a child—loving and being loved without question.

When I leave this province I shall visit you, and then, perhaps, my well-beloved Lucius, "thou half of my soul," I may be able to make this plain to you, and prepare you to see this wondrous light even as Mary prepared me.

There is no doubt, dear friend, that in *her* the perfection of the new life is fully manifest. It is a revelation merely to see her face shining with love, with unbounded, overflowing love, but love in which everything carnal has been transcended. It is wonderful to see her as she sits at the feet of the Master, filled and thrilled with his love, and in her eyes the peace of God that passes all understanding.

The next day being the Sabbath, the Master went out from the house, taking Peter, John, and James with him; but, after going a little distance he withdrew by himself to pray, leaving the three to watch and keep the people from disturbing him. It is probable that in these periods of prayer and communion with his God, the Master receives and replenishes his superhuman powers.

An immense crowd came out from Jerusalem to Bethany, for the news of the raising of Lazarus had quickly spread, and people were curious to see what a resurrected man looked like, and if possible to hear his experiences. Lazarus bore the infliction beautifully, but, as he could only tell the visitors what he had told us, they were naturally much disappointed. Many sick people also were brought out, and when the Master returned from prayer he healed them all. Some of those who crowded about him and touched the hem of his garment were healed without a word being spoken. It is marvelous what power resides in this man, and it can come from nowhere but from the one God, who has made and who preserves all things.

Many of those who came out from the city believed and acknowledged the Master as a prophet sent from God; but others, whom I recognized as prominent Pharisees and Sadducees, members of the Sanhedrim, stood aloof and seemed to consult with each other. I did not like their attitude, and so sent Syrus to find out what they were talking about. He overheard them say that the Master's miracles were done by the power of Beelzebub in order to mislead the people of Israel; that no true prophet would act as a physician on the Sabbath, and break other ordinances, as Jesus did; and that, if he continued in his wicked course, some great evil would befall God's Temple and people. As I thought of Saul of Tarsus and of his whole-souled hatred, I began to fear for the Master's safety in the midst of such bitter enemies.

Syrus has also renewed his acquaintance with Judas of Kerioth. They have talked much together, and the faithful rascal, knowing how I am interested in what concerns the Master, has reported to me all that Judas said. It seems that the Master, for some time after the Baptist's death, wandered about in Syro-Phœnicia and the Decapolis, as if to keep out of Herod's dominions. There he had healed and converted many of the Gentiles, much to Judas's disgust, who thought that the Master was making himself entirely too common. Then Jesus, with John, James, and Peter, went up privately to the Feast of Tabernacles. But when he was in Jerusalem, he openly taught in the Temple, arousing great hostility among the leading Pharisees and Sadducees, because he spoke against their vices—said they were the children of the devil, and proclaimed himself to be the Son of God. Once he declared, "Before Abraham was—I am," and the enraged Jews took up stones to cast at him, but he passed through them in the same mysterious way as at the Sea of Galilee.

This hostility was, if anything, greater when he came up in the winter to the Feast of Dedication, and preached in Solomon's porch. Here he not only reiterated his claim of being the Son of God, but added that he and the Father were one. And again he had to use his mysterious powers to escape.

Since then he had been keeping out of the province of Judea, going about from place to place, sending out his disciples to preach, and talking to them about the Kingdom of Heaven.

THE KINGDOM OF HEAVEN

Judas had not been able to make out exactly what sort of a kingdom Jesus meant to bring about, and could not understand why he did not act at once, while so many were enthusiastic about him, instead of wandering about the country like a vagabond, and turning away rich men who would have followed him if he had not required them to sell all their goods and give the proceeds to the poor. He had also talked about his being obliged to suffer many things, to be rejected by this generation, and to lay down his life. He had said, to be sure, that no one could take it away from him, but he would lay it down himself, and that he had the power to lay it down and to take it again. Judas did not doubt the Master could do this, but he could not see what good could come of any such performance.

All of the twelve had worried considerably about this, and one day Peter asked him what were they going to get who had given up everything and followed him. And the Master replied, that they would be repaid a hundredfold in lands, houses, and wealth, and besides would have everlasting life. As for the chief disciples, they would sit on twelve thrones and judge the twelve tribes of Israel. Then, just when they were beginning to feel a little more encouraged, the Master went on to say that they would be persecuted and killed for his sake, and would look for him and would not find him, and that he was going away, tho he would come again.

"And in short," said Syrus, at the conclusion of his tale, "it is easy to see that Judas, tho he does not speak of leaving the Master, is very much dissatisfied. I suppose he feels as I did—that a man who has such supernatural powers ought to use them, if not for himself, then for the glory of Israel and for the advantage of his faithful followers, and not put them off with promises and puzzle them with mysterious talk."

"I imagine that Judas does not find the post of treasurer up to his expectations."

"I should say not," cried Syrus. "Judas says that often the common purse is absolutely empty, and that, whenever it is filled by some generous gift, the Master squanders it upon the poor without a thought of where their next meal is to come from. He says that the Lady of Magdala has practically given her entire income to the Master, and so have several other women, but it has all been wasted. And then," added Syrus, in a significant tone, "Judas, you know, was at one time much taken with the Lady of Magdala, and I do not think he has ever recovered from it. You should have seen the look on his face last night, when she sat at the Master's feet and never took her eyes from him. Judas is a keen man, but he has a strange disposition."

"That will do, Syrus," I said, not relishing the turn his talk had taken. "You are invaluable. Continue to keep your eyes and ears open, and to keep me informed. I would not have anything happen to the Master for worlds."

In the evening, the crowd returned to Jerusalem, and Jesus continued his teaching to the little circle in the court. He talked now of vast and mysterious things, of the one, eternal God, and of the Father, Son, and Holy Spirit. Among other things, he said that no one could come to the Father but through him, that the Father was in him and he in the Father, that whoever had seen him had seen the Father, and that he would be with us always, even to the end of the world.

The teaching of the night before I had understood perfectly, it was so clear and practical; but this is beyond me, and I think beyond all of us. The Master saw it and said with his immeasurable sweetness:

"You think these are hard sayings; and so they are *now*, but when I go away they will become plain."

"But you must not leave us," cried Peter impetuously. "We can not suffer it. What would become of us without our Master?"

"It is expedient that I go away, for, if I do not go away, the Holy Spirit will not come to you. And through the Holy Spirit you will understand all these things." And then, having blessed us, he retired to his chamber.

The next morning the Master and his disciples returned to Peræa, and, in the afternoon, I took leave of my kind hostesses, who, however, urged me to remain till the Master returned for the Passover. But I felt it my duty, now that I was well, to return and report myself to my superior officer and uncle. So with much regret I left the dwelling where were spent the most marvelous days of my life—nay, rather, where my old life ended and my new life began. Now, do not laugh, my Lucius, I believe I can make it all clear to you when I see you.

By the way, I have forgotten to tell you about Syrus and Susanna. Before the Master left, I spoke to Mary, and, as I expected, she made no objection, but, on the contrary, was delighted for my sake as well as theirs.

"You see, Caius," she said, "you are reaping the reward of your unselfish deeds. Kindness begets kindness and love begets love."

"But do you think Syrus is fit for even Susanna?" I asked, to turn the conversation.

"Why not? Do you think that a man who has shown such unselfish and tireless devotion to you is not capable of a true and constant love for such a dear child as Susanna?"

"But he is such a graceless unbeliever."

"He will believe, he *must* believe, in the Master. He, whose soul is filled with such love for a man, must in time come to feel the love of God and of his Son. And Susanna will aid him."

"Syrus has his good points," I admitted.

Mary told the Master of the intended marriage, and asked permission to bring the couple before him that he might bless them. Syrus came somewhat unwillingly. In fact, he had kept as much as possible out of the Master's sight since his arrival. When Jesus saw him he said:

"You were one of those who followed me in Galilee, because of the loaves and fishes."

"Yes, Master," murmured Syrus.

"And you wished to obtain some place of power in my kingdom."

Syrus bowed his head.

"But when you heard me say that my kingdom was not of this world, you, like so many others, left me."

Syrus covered his face with his hands.

"Do not grieve," said the Master in a comforting tone. "You did what you thought best. Did I not say to you that no man could come unto me except it were given to him by the Father? And in the Father's own good time you will come."

THE KINGDOM OF HEAVEN

Then he blessed them and their future union, and the two withdrew—Syrus being glad enough to escape from the Master's searching gaze.

Mary and I have arranged that the marriage shall take place after the Passover, when the crowds have departed and the city has become quiet again, so that nothing may occur to mar the festivities. I believe Mary is right; the influence of Susanna is making itself felt, for in many ways Syrus is quite a different fellow already.

On my return to Jerusalem both Pilate and my aunt Claudia were overjoyed to see me looking so well and happy, as they had heard such a terrible account of my disease from the lieutenant who had gone on with the prisoners. I told them in full the story of the past two days, and I think that my aunt is almost ready to believe in the Master's divine mission, and would believe, if she had an opportunity of hearing him; for you must know that she has become a Jewish proselyte.

Pilate smiled at my enthusiasm, and said that in about a month the old Roman in me would rise again and put an end to my new Jewish notions. But, as far as he could see, there was nothing dangerous in the Nazarene's spiritual kingdom. In fact, with its doctrine of non-resistance, it was quite an improvement on the rigid intolerance of the Pharisees, who had given him nothing but trouble since he had come to Judea, and who were now doing all they could to get him into difficulties with the proprætor Vitellius, and even with the divine Cæsar. He promised that, as far as was consistent with his own safety, he would try to protect the foolish prophet from the machinations of his enemies, and he would have no objection to anything reasonable that I might do in that matter; so he put me in command of the garrison of the Antonia.

As I entered my quarters I found waiting for me a Jew with his face covered, who said he wanted to see me in secret.

"What is it you wish?" I asked when we were alone.

"Will you promise not to reveal who I am or what I tell you to any of the Jews?"

I promised, and he uncovered his face, disclosing the features of one of the most prominent Pharisees of Jerusalem.

"My name is Nicodemus," he said, "and I am a member of the council of the Sanhedrim. We had a meeting to-day, and the matter of Lazarus and Jesus of Nazareth was discussed. The majority, who are Sadducees, think that if Jesus continues to draw people unto him he may arouse in you Romans the fear of a revolt, and so you may be led to oppress us more harshly and even destroy us. The high priest, Caiaphas, was very violent, and said it was expedient that one man should die for the people so that the whole nation might not perish. And, as that idea pleased most of the Sanhedrists, they resolved to compass the death of the Nazarene in any way they could. The great difficulty is, that they are afraid of the people if they attack him openly, for many are devoted to him; and besides, even if they could apprehend him, our council has not the power of putting him to death. Pontius Pilate has given them no satisfaction when they have approached him in this matter. Now I

have learned that you were healed by Jesus.
Is this true?"

"It is."

"For that reason I come to you. You have
great influence with the procurator, and I ask
you to do what you can to protect Jesus. Do
you believe on him?"

"I believe he is a great and good man with
wondrous powers from God."

"I believe the same, altho I have not yet acknowledged it openly—on account of my position.
Besides the wisdom of being prudent for my
own sake, I feel that I can be of more assistance
to him in secret than if I declared my belief,
which would insure my immediate expulsion
from the Sanhedrim. Not long ago, when they
were discussing the same question, I ventured
to make a mild plea for common justice—that
they should not condemn a man before they had
heard him—and they nearly tore me in pieces."

"I understand."

"So I can count on you?"

"I give you my word. There shall not be a
hair of his head touched if I can prevent it."

THE KINGDOM OF HEAVEN

Then Nicodemus gave me the names of those who were most violent against the Master, and once more pledging me to keep the matter secret— even from Pilate—covered up his face and slipped out into the darkness.

I fear for the Master's safety, my Lucius,

"Such power of ill doth move the bigot's arm." *

I know that he is possessed of unearthly powers and, so far, has been able to protect himself from his enemies. Yet this secret, malicious plotting makes me dread that some treacherous fanatic may take him unawares—and—it needs only an instant to kill.

Write soon, my Lucius, and make an offering to the gods for your friend's recovery. Farewell.

---

* Tantum religio potuit suadere malorum.—*Lucretius.*

XVIII
Impending Danger

XVIII

At Jerusalem

ALMOST two weeks have passed, my Lucius, since I wrote you last. When I have been off duty, my time has been mostly spent with Mary and Martha at Bethany. You would not be interested much in our conversations, as they have been altogether about the Master, his acts and his sayings. Lazarus visits his sisters frequently, sometimes bringing with him a young cousin named John, the son of one of the more liberal or Hellenizing Jews, who has Grecianized his name, Simon, into Simonides. The father is quite a wealthy merchant and made his fortune in Ephesus, but, like many others of his race, has returned to Jerusalem to end his days on holy ground. The son, who is a very intelligent and enthusiastic youth, came to believe on Jesus at the Feast of Tabernacles; and was present

with his father at the raising of Lazarus. As
he, too, has a Hellenistic tendency, he has added
the name of Markos to his own and prefers to be
called by it. I mentioned him especially because he was able to oblige me in a certain matter
I shall tell you of.

You remember Nicodemus? Well, a few days
after his first visit, he returned privately with
another Sanhedrist, named Joseph of Arimathea,
who also believes on the Master—secretly, of
course—and who had knowledge of some further
facts in connection with the plot against him.
Among other things, there had been talk of putting Lazarus to death also—as many had believed
because of his resurrection. These two Jews
are very earnest, and I hope with their aid to
protect the Master as far as I can; that is, as far as
he will allow me, for his ways are past finding out.

As soon as I could I hastened up to Bethany,
where I found Lazarus with Markos and told
him of the danger, without mentioning who my
informants were. Lazarus smiled when he heard
of the plot against him and said:

"I shall take no thought of this, Caius Claudius.

IMPENDING DANGER

A man who has passed through the portals of
the grave and has returned can not fear death.
I am ready to go again at any time."

But Markos volunteered to take a message
from me to the Master, who was then not far
from the Jordan, in Peræa. On his return, he
told me that the Master had thanked both him
and me for our kindness, but had added:
"I shall go up to Jerusalem, and all those things
shall be accomplished which are written by the
prophets about the Son of Man."

So you see he knows the danger and yet is determined to proceed. It may be that he sees before him a greater victory, because of the greater
danger, or, perhaps, he may wish to terminate
his career by a glorious death. It is certain that
there is no fear in him, tho I must confess myself
utterly unable to understand the motives that
direct his actions. They are beyond me—may be
above me.

The Master and the twelve chief disciples arrived
in Bethany yesterday, and are accommodated
in Martha's house. Accompanying them were
his mother, her sister, also named Mary, who

is the mother of John and James, another Mary who is the wife of a certain Cleopas, and a sweet-faced woman named Salome, very different, tho, from her vicious little royal namesake. These are now occupying Lazarus' house in the city, where Martha is hostess, while Mary remains in Bethany, to take care of the Master and his disciples.

Markos tells me that, to celebrate their arrival, there was a feast at the house of a certain Simon, whom Jesus had healed of leprosy. It was a sort of village affair, with a large number of guests, including both Markos and Lazarus. In the midst of the feast, Mary, wishing to show special honor to the Master, and probably recalling her former action at Capernaum, entered the room with an alabastron of precious spikenard, which she poured over his head, and then knelt down at the foot of his couch. Some of the disciples, Markos says, murmured, and Judas spoke out quite sharply:

"What good is this waste of precious ointment? It might have been sold for more than three hundred denarii and given to the poor."

IMPENDING DANGER

But the Master turned to him and spoke with great solemnity:

"Let her alone. Why do you trouble her? She has wrought a good work on me. For you will always have the poor with you, and you can help them whenever you desire; but you will not always have me. She has done what she could; she has anointed beforehand my body for its burial. And wherever these good tidings shall be preached throughout the whole world, what she has done shall be told as a memorial of her."

So Judas was silenced, but Markos says that he took it quite hard, and soon after left the feast. He thinks that Judas must dislike Mary, for everything she does seems to displease him. I think I know the reason, and I can not see why the Master chose him as one of the twelve. He does not seem to comprehend the real meaning of the doctrine any better than Syrus. But, as I said, the Master's ways are past finding out. There is much that I do not understand myself, and his favorite disciples often appear puzzled. Mary alone seems—not to comprehend, but, I might say—to feel, what he means. It is certain that she always manages to do what he approves of. Hers must be the intuition of unselfish, spiritual, perfect love.

To-day I went over to greet the Master. He was surrounded by a multitude of those who had known him in Galilee and those drawn from the city by curiosity to see the man who had risen from the dead and the wonder-worker who had raised him. Jesus made me sit down by him, while he went on with his teaching, which was in the simplest language possible, but full of the deepest thought, and interspersed with exquisite parables. These were evidently made up as he talked, yet were as perfect in form as the best fables of Æsop, and of a meaning far more profound; but so simple that, after once hearing, you can not forget them. You remember I sent you one I heard at Capernaum. Well, I shall write these out, as well as others I may hear, and, after the Master returns to Galilee, I shall send you the whole collection. Even if you do not believe the doctrines they illustrate, you will appreciate them as little literary masterpieces.

IMPENDING DANGER

I came back with Markos over the Mount of
Olives and through the valley of the brook
Kedron. The whole country round about is
filled with the multitudes that have come from
all parts to this, the greatest of the Jewish feasts.
All the houses in the city and in the suburbs are
crowded, and the hillsides are dotted with num-
berless tents. The city gates are left open at
night, for, during the feast, the surrounding
country for quite a distance is considered, for
religious purposes, as part of the city, and free
egress and ingress must be allowed, as important
services in the Temple are to take place at all
hours of the day and night.

The Master said that he would come in to-
morrow to visit the Temple. I am quite anxious,
tho Nicodemus tells me that he does not believe
the Sanhedrists will attempt to do anything
openly—on account of the multitude of Galileans
that are here, but will try to take him unawares.
It will not be a bad idea to send a small detachment of soldiers out to Bethany and Syrus along
with them. He will be glad enough of the mission
—on account of Susanna, you know—and then

his keen scent will surely ferret out any underhand work that may be attempted. But the Master must not know of it, as he might be offended. I wish he would be more cautious. Yet I shall leave undone nothing that is in my power to protect him. Farewell.

XIX
The Son of David

XIX

At Jerusalem

THE Master entered the city to-day, my
Lucius, but in a way I had never imagined.
It was indeed a strange affair.

Early in the morning I was awakened by great
shouts in the streets and outside of the walls.
Going to the battlements of the Tower, I looked
out and saw a vast multitude streaming from the
Jericho gate, bearing palm branches in their
hands and shouting, "Hosanna to the Son of
David!" Their shouts were answered by another
multitude, coming down the road from Bethany:
they, also, were waving palm branches, and in
front of them, riding on an ass, was a man whom
I knew must be the Master. My heart sank
within me, as I thought of the possible danger,
since it would not take much, should the priests

attempt to interfere, to turn that enthusiastic multitude into a raging mob. As the two jubilant hosts met, those coming from the city stood on either side and spread their garments on the road before the Master, waved their palm branches, and continued shouting hosannas. When he had passed they fell in behind the procession.

I gave orders quickly, and, before the multitude entered the city, had strong bodies of troops posted in the side streets on the way to the Temple with strict orders not to interfere, except in case of open violence. I led a cohort myself to the gate of the outer court, called the "Court of the Gentiles." Just as I was leaving the Tower, an officer came in hot haste from Pilate, to order the very thing I had done. But our display of force was unnecessary. The crowd, tho wild with enthusiasm, kept perfect order, and I suppose the priests and the Pharisees were awed by the immense numbers of the Master's followers, whose unorganized shouts finally settled into a species of regular chant. I could hear it distinctly as they came across the great bridge, which is the main approach to the Temple:

THE SON OF DAVID

"Hosanna, hosanna to the Son of David!
   Blessed is the King that cometh in the name of the Lord!
   Even the King of Israel. Hosanna in the highest!"

And then they appeared, the Master with his face calm and serene—the multitude fairly crazed with joyous enthusiasm. I noticed also, as they came nearer, that the faces of the disciples glowed with triumph, and the eyes of Judas, especially, flashed exultant. At the gate the Master dismounted and entered the outer court, followed by as many of the people as could crowd within. With a small guard, I took up a position where I could command the whole place.

The Master stood on the terrace of the great building that contains the inner courts, and looked about him. Behind him were the scowling faces of the priests, and before him the tables of the money-changers and the seats of those that sell doves for the sacrifices. The place is usually a scene of noisy chaffering, but now every one was hushed and expectant, wondering what this strange being would do.

For a while he stood there silent, gazing about him; then the serene face changed, lighted up by a godlike wrath. His eyes flashed, and, with a voice that quivered with indignation, he cried:

"Is it not written, 'My house shall be called a house of prayer'? But you have made it a den of thieves!"

And, without another word, he walked majestically to the table of the nearest money-changer and overturned it. Leaving the terrified tradesman to scramble for his scattered coins, he proceeded to the next, while the multitude looked on in dumb amazement. But before he reached the third, a panic fear took possession of the crowd of traffickers, and, sweeping the coins into their money-bags, gathering the bird-cages together, or driving their cattle before them, they stumbled over each other in their wild haste to escape.

One of the priests came up to me and asked:

"Sir Officer, are you going to allow this?"

"I see no cause for interference."

"But the procurator has ordered that we be protected."

"And my orders are not to interfere unless there is actual violence, and those fellows seem to be leaving of their own accord. In fact, I think your

CHRIST ENTERING JERUSALEM, from the painting by Paul Gustave Doré

"*Hosanna, hosanna to the son of David! Blessed is the King that cometh in the name of the Lord! Even the King of Israel. Hosanna in the highest!*"

Temple will be all the better when cleansed of that rubbish, tho perhaps the profits of Annas and Caiaphas may be diminished."

"I shall report this to Pilate," he muttered, as he turned away.

It was amazing, the power of that man! Not one of the traders ventured to resist him, and the vast crowd kept absolutely quiet, awed by his look.

Then, when the court was cleared of the vulgar traders, the Master returned to the top of the terrace. There he taught the people, and they, as usual, brought to him numbers of sick and infirm, whom he healed, and little children, whom he blessed.

The crowd that listened to him was quiet and reverent, so there was not the slightest need for my troops. I remained, however, entranced by the beautiful precepts and the exquisite parables. Toward the close of day he told the crowd to depart, saying that he would be in the same place on the morrow, and then with his disciples went quietly away to Bethany.

This man is incomprehensible to me, my Lucius.

UNDER PONTIUS PILATE

His control of those vast masses of excited Jews was simply marvelous. But, why, after his triumphal entry and that magnificent display of power in the Temple, should he depart so quietly? —I can not understand. It is not what one would expect from any man—but, is it what a god would do? I do not know. Farewell.

XX
Denunciation

XX

At Jerusalem

FOR three days, my Lucius, I have been filled with anxiety. The entire city is seething underneath, tho everything is quiet enough on the surface. I have feared that, at any moment, there might be a clash between the enthusiastic followers of the Nazarene and the Sadducee priests and the Pharisees, whose hatred deepens every moment. This can plainly be seen in the dark looks they cast at the Master as he passes on his way to and from the Temple, where, through the day, he spends his time preaching and healing. But each evening he returns to Bethany. By the way, the money-changers and the dove-sellers asked if they might establish themselves outside of the Temple, and to this he made no objection. Pilate also tells me that every day he has to listen to deputations from the Pharisees and the priests urging him to arrest Jesus, but he has put them off, saying that he has his officers on the watch, and it will be time enough to act when anything seditious occurs. Rabbis have frequently taught in the Temple, and he is not well enough acquainted with the Jewish religion to know or care whether this particular rabbi belongs to one of their accepted sects, or is trying to start a new one. So he told them to settle their disputes among themselves, and not to trouble him with their theological subtleties.

I think my good uncle is rather enjoying the discomfiture of the Pharisees as a sort of repayment for the trouble they gave him about those standards I wrote you of. But I do not like their persistence. Constant dropping of water wears away the hardest rocks, and my good uncle, tho hard enough at times, has several weak spots—especially when fear for his own safety is aroused. Then he is liable to act hastily and without the best judgment. I am glad that he put me in charge of the garrison, and I only hope he will not change his mind.

These persistent Pharisees and Sadducees, who

DENUNCIATION

now seem at last united in their common hatred
of the Master, are trying in every way to entrap
him and are asking him all sorts of hard questions,
which he answers in the cleverest fashion, often
turning their questions back upon themselves,
and so confounding them. Markos tells me
that, day before yesterday, the priests asked
the Master by what authority he had cleared
the Temple and now taught in it. And he, instead of answering, asked them another question,
"Was the baptism of John from God or not?"
This was a poser, because if they said "yes,"
they would have to recognize Jesus's authority,
since John had acknowledged him as the Christ,
and had sent his disciples to him; and if they said
"no," they would have the multitude against them,
for many of those who do not believe in Jesus
believe, like Saul of Tarsus, that John was a true
prophet. So the priests had to acknowledge that
they could not answer him, and then the Master
said, "Neither will I tell you by what authority
I do these things." You see he has as good a
rabbinical training as the keenest of them. And
yesterday when I was in the Temple, inspecting the

guard—we keep a whole cohort there during the feasts—a group of Sadducees and Pharisees came up to Jesus, and their leader said:

"Master, we know that you are true and teach the way of God in truth and care not for any one; for you are no respecter of persons. Tell us then what you think of this: Is it lawful to give tribute to Cæsar or not?"

You see this was a pretty hard question. If he said "yes," he would lose favor with his Galileans, who hate the tribute above all things; and if he said "no," there would be a good reason for Pilate to arrest him. But the Master looked up with a smile and replied:

"Why do you tempt me, you hypocrites? Show me the tribute money."

So they handed him a denarius, and he asked in the most innocent way:

"Whose image and superscription is this?"

"Cæsar's."

Then, handing back the coin, he said:

"Render unto Cæsar the things that are Cæsar's, and unto God the things that are God's."

They slunk away, feeling cheap enough, but

not loving him any the more for beating them at their own game. But I wish the Master would not talk so much about them or would not denounce them with such terrible earnestness. I shall breathe much more freely when this feast is over, and he is safe back in his own Galilee.

The whole tenor of his philippics is so different from the precepts of universal love and forgiveness I have hitherto heard from him, that I can not understand why he speaks thus, unless he is actually courting an attack from his foes. If this is his purpose, he is doing the proper thing—I myself would grow bitter under such a terrible arraignment—and there is no doubt that the opposition to him is rapidly coming to a head. I feel it in the air. To-day he was particularly cutting in his denunciation. I remember most of it—it seemed to burn itself into my soul:

"Wo unto you, Scribes and Pharisees, hypocrites!" he said, "for you shut up the Kingdom of Heaven against men; for you neither go in yourselves nor suffer those that are entering to go in.

"Wo unto you, Scribes and Pharisees, hypocrites! for you devour widows' houses, and for a pretense make long prayers; therefore you shall receive the greater damnation.

"Wo unto you, Scribes and Pharisees, hypocrites! for you compass sea and land to make one proselyte, and when he is made you make him tenfold more the child of Sheol than yourselves.

"Wo unto you, Scribes and Pharisees, hypocrites! for you pay tithe of mint and anise and cummin, and have left undone the weightier matters of the law, judgment and mercy and faith; these ought you to have done, and not leave the other undone. You blind guides, that strain at a gnat and swallow a camel!

"Wo unto you, Scribes and Pharisees, hypocrites! for you make clean the outside of the cup and platter, but within they are full of extortion and excess. You blind Pharisees, cleanse first that which is within the cup and the platter, that the outside of them may be clean also.

"Wo unto you, Scribes and Pharisees, hypocrites! for you are like unto whited sepulchers, which indeed appear beautiful outside, but are within full of dead men's bones and all uncleanness. Even so you also outwardly appear righteous unto men, but within you are full of hypocrisy and iniquity.

"Wo unto you, Scribes and Pharisees, hypocrites! because you build the tombs of the prophets and beautify the sepulchers of the righteous and say, 'If we had lived in the days of our fathers we would not have been partakers with them in the blood of the prophets.' Wherefore you bear witness to yourselves that you are the children of them who killed the prophets. Fill up then the measure of your fathers. Serpents, generation of vipers, how can you escape the damnation of Gehenna?

"Wherefore, behold, I send unto you prophets and wise men and scribes; and some of them you shall kill and crucify, and some of them you shall scourge in your synagogs, and persecute from city to city; that upon you may come all the righteous blood shed upon the earth, from the blood of righteous Abel unto the blood of Zacharias, son of Barachias, whom you slew between the temple and the altar. Verily, I say unto you, all these things shall come upon this generation."

As he spoke he reminded me of John the Baptist prophesying on the heights of Machærus, only Jesus was grander. He looked like some avenging deity, about to bring destruction upon mankind for their sins.

But at the end his features softened into an infinite tenderness. You could hear the tears in his voice as he said:

"O Jerusalem, Jerusalem, thou that killest the prophets, and stonest them that are sent unto thee, how often would I have gathered thy children together, even as a hen gathers her chickens under her wings, and you would not! Behold, your house is left unto you desolate!"

Then he made his way quietly through the crowd, and, followed by his disciples, returned to Bethany.

This evening Herod entered the city. He has just returned from Rome, where he went to beg aid from Cæsar against Aretas, who still continues to worry him by border raids, tho I suppose he docs not dare to make a regular invasion of the territory of one of Cæsar's tributary kinglets. Herod will stay here for a few days, as of course he would not let slip this opportunity of currying favor with his pious subjects, by keeping the Passover in the midst of the thousands who have come from Galilee and Peræa.

Herod and Pilate are yet somewhat at outs, as Pilate, like Vitellius, had refused him aid. And my uncle has had news from Rome that what Herod said to Cæsar about him was not particularly favorable, as was natural. And so the two rulers are treating each other with the most distinguished and distant consideration. Herod sent a formal embassy to announce his approach and to pay his respects to the representative of the divine Cæsar in Jerusalem, and Pilate sent me with a troop of horse, to escort the tetrarch to his lodgings in a style befitting his petty majesty.

Herod, as usual, was most affable, and made me remain and partake of the supper which had been prepared for them. Herodias also made herself quite entertaining, while the little demon, Salome, sat demurely silent, occasionally looking at me with a knowing look, as much as to say, "You see, my wise Roman, that a little Jewish princess can sometimes manage to attain her end without your honorable aid." But she did not in the least bother the "wise Roman," who had learned that his old wisdom was folly, and was now acquiring a new wisdom that was far beyond her little power to fathom.

In the course of our conversation, Herod asked me:

"Do you know anything about this new prophet, Jesus of Nazareth, whom I have heard so much of lately?"

"He is at present preaching daily in Jerusalem."

"Have you heard him?"

"Several times."

"Is he as great an orator as John the Baptizer?"

"Much greater."

"I should like to hear him. And I must send for him to come and give me a specimen of his art."

"He is to be found in the Temple every day."

"Well, I certainly must secure him before I leave the city."

I wonder if the Master would come, and if he came what he would say. I wonder if he would denounce Herodias as John did, and if he would

crush the precocious Salome? Or would he—
with his wondrous power and his unerring insight
into the secrets of human hearts—take these two
royal sinners, as he did Mary of Magdala, and
convert their perverted and diabolical sensuality
into pure and spiritual love. I wonder if it is
possible—yet all things seem to be possible to him.
And, my Lucius, I should like to be there to see.
Farewell.

XXI
The Passover

XXI

At Jerusalem

TO-NIGHT is the beginning of the Passover, for the Jewish day begins at sunset. From the battlements I can see, all over the town, the bright sparkle of the lights in the rooms where the feast is being celebrated, and, through the valleys and on the sides of the hills, the dimmer glow of the tents of the pilgrims. It is very impressive—the whole nation celebrating its deliverance from servitude in Egypt in the simple faith that their God is still watching over them. From Herod in his luxurious lodgings, down to the Galilean fisherman in his tent, the same psalms are being sung, the same prayers uttered, the same blessings said. It is a wondrous thing, my Lucius, this absorption of a whole people in the worship of one spiritual God, and it makes me believe that had we Romans such a religion—that is, a belief in a universal spirit—instead of our shallow polytheism, there would not be the skepticism and unbelief that have eaten the heart out of our worship. Think of divine honors being paid to such a one as now degrades Capreæ! Yet such things are the natural outcome of our state religion. But this worship of the universal Father—especially as it is set forth by the Master —is impregnable to any assaults of the wisest philosophy. Even your lofty Stoicism must retire defeated.

For two days the Master has not been seen in the city. Since his bitter words against the Scribes and Pharisees, he has not shown his face, and both friends and foes are inquiring about him. I myself was quite anxious until this afternoon when Syrus came in from Bethany and told me that Jesus had remained in and near that village ever since he came back that evening. All day yesterday he was with the twelve in a garden called Gethsemane, belonging to Simonides, and situated on the near slope of the Mount of Olives. When they came home the disciples all looked very sober and solemn. The first part of last night the Master had spent in that same garden in prayer, accompanied by only Peter, John, and James. Syrus, with some of the guard, had followed them to Gethsemane, but there was no sign of any one prowling about. He has also talked with some of the Master's enemies and is pretty sure that they are not likely to attempt anything during the feast, as there are so many Galileans here. The tremendous demonstration on the day after last Sabbath has really alarmed them. Still, he thinks it well to be on our guard, for tho the Master is perfectly able to protect himself, if he wants to, yet he has such strange ideas that there is no telling what danger he may deliberately walk into.

Syrus came into the city this afternoon with Judas, whom the Master had sent to purchase something for the feast to be celebrated somewhere in the city to-night. Syrus thinks that he has shown a little sense in keeping this matter quiet, for even Judas does not know the place. On the way Judas grew quite confidential under Syrus's skilful manipulation, and told him that he was beginning to be dissatisfied with the Mas-

ter's service. According to Judas's way of thinking, the fact that Jesus, with superhuman powers at
his command, with almost the entire population
of Jerusalem hailing him as King, and with his
enemies fleeing before his mere glance, had not
availed himself of such an opportunity of estab-
lishing his kingdom—but instead had dropped
back into his old business of healing and telling
stories—either showed that the Master was not
what he claimed to be, or that he did not have
the courage or patriotism needed for his mission.
It was hard to believe that such a one could be
the Messiah. And then, after his scathing de-
nunciations of the Scribes and Pharisees, he had
led his disciples aside on the Mount of Olives
and had told them all sorts of discouraging things.
He had predicted the destruction of the Temple
and of the city, had said that he himself was likely
to be taken and slain, that his disciples would
suffer all sorts of persecutions for his sake, and
even be tortured and put to death. This seemed
to Judas a shabby ending to the glorious tales
Jesus had told them of his kingdom, when he had
seduced them into giving up their all and follow-

ing.him. To be sure, he had promised that at the end of the world—whose dreadful termination he had vividly described—he would come in clouds with hosts of angels and raise them into the highest heavens in life eternal. But while that might do for foolish ex-hetairai like Mary, whom he had completely fascinated, or for silly milksops like John, or shallow boasters like Peter, it did not appeal to men of common sense who had a little worldly wisdom left, and who knew something of the true value of money and the proper use of power.

Syrus asked Judas if he intended leaving the Master. Judas turned pale and replied that he had not made up his mind yet. Perhaps the Master knew what was best, and might be waiting for the close of the festival before he would act— anyhow, he would wait and see. And at the gate he and Syrus had parted.

It is quite amusing to notice how Judas has lately fallen in Syrus's estimation. As I wrote you, Syrus is now quite a different person. But, even if Susanna had not so deeply affected him, if he were his old self, he always did have one unshakeable virtue—faithfulness. He is so devoted to me that he is ready to do anything for those I love, as well as for me. And so, tho I know he can not have as much understanding of the Master as Judas, yet he despises the latter, because he speaks against the man he is serving, and now he trusts him as little as I do.

It was Syrus's idea that I should post him and a small detachment of soldiers to-night at the Jericho gate, so that, when the Master and his disciples entered, they might follow them and guard the house where they supped. And just now he came in and reported that the Master had celebrated the Passover in the house of Markos's father, that there had been no signs of danger, and that a little before midnight the disciples had sung the final song and had departed with the Master on the road to Bethany. He had followed them a little way, and then had left the guard at the gate to question strictly any one who might wish to go out.

By the way, he also told me that Judas had left the house in the middle of the feast, and that he had accosted him and asked where he was going.

THE PASSOVER

And Judas had replied that the Master had sent him on an errand, telling him to do it quickly. Then he had hurried away into the city. Syrus blamed himself for not following him, and asked permission to go to Bethany to assure himself of the Master's safety. So I let him go, just as the trumpets sounded from the Temple to announce the midnight opening of the sanctuary gates for the preparation of the morrow's festive sacrifice.

I left this letter, which I have been scribbling at intervals during the evening, and looked out over the city and the valley to the encircling hills. All lights are now extinguished, and the full moon is pouring a silver flood over the sleeping earth. There is absolute stillness. Everything seems the embodiment of perfect peace. And yet I feel strangely disturbed. I wish Syrus were back with news of the Master's safe arrival in Bethany. The keen, repellent face of Judas keeps coming before my mind. If Syrus had only followed him!

However, my Lucius, I shall try to go to sleep and shall write you more in the morning.

XXII

Before Pilate

XXII

At Jerusalem

WHAT we dreaded has happened, even while we were taking measures to prevent it. The Master has been betrayed and is even now hanging on the cross outside the city walls. I can not realize it. That pure and noble man, that lofty prophet sent from God, is suffering the fate that seems to be the due of every great soul who tries to make his degraded fellow-men abandon their evil ways and become like him. It was so with Valerius, with Socrates, with the Gracchi, and now with one who transcends them all. After all, *homo homini lupus* must be true. Let me try, as coherently as possible, to tell you the wretched tale.

When I ceased writing to you a little after midnight, I went to bed and tossed about, half awake and half asleep, a prey to disjointed visions.

UNDER PONTIUS PILATE

The faces of Judas and the Master whirled about me, driving me distracted by the rapidity of their transformations. At last I was aroused by a slave, who said that Syrus and some others wanted to see me immediately. In the antechamber I found Syrus with Mary, Lazarus, and Markos, all weeping and lamenting that the Master had been betrayed and was in the hands of the priests, who might even now be killing him. Overwhelmed as I was by the terrible news, it was some time before I could make out any definite story. But this is what I finally elicited:

Syrus, after charging the guard at the gate with my instructions, had hurried along the road to Bethany. He passed Gethsemane, but, as all seemed quiet, he did not in his haste go in. But it seems that the Master and his disciples were there, tho most of them were probably asleep. When Syrus reached Bethany, he roused Lazarus and Mary, to find that Jesus had not returned. Filled with alarm, he took the detachment of soldiers, and, accompanied by Lazarus and Mary, started back along the road, looking for the Master and his disciples on every side.

BEFORE PILATE

As they came into the vale of Kedron they saw a large body of men with torches entering the Temple gate, and, just afterward, Lazarus was hailed by Markos, who was hiding naked in the bushes. Lazarus gave him his cloak, and Markos then came forth and told them that, some time after the Master and his disciples had left his father's house and he was asleep, he was aroused by a knocking at the door. He hastily threw a sheet about him, went down, and found Judas, who asked if the Master were still there. On being informed that he had departed, Judas turned away, and then Markos saw, a little way up the street, a band of troops and a crowd of men with swords and clubs and torches. Seeing Judas join them, and being filled with apprehension, he did not dare to wait to dress, but followed after them just as he was. They went out of the Jericho gate, the guard not questioning them, as the officer in command of the troops showed them a paper. Markos followed in the crowd and so passed through. Judas led them straight to Gethsemane, and there, inside the gate, they found most of the disciples asleep.

UNDER PONTIUS PILATE

As they were questioning them, the Master came out from the recesses of the garden with Peter and James and John, and immediately Judas ran up to him and kissed him, and said "Hail, Rabbi!" And the Master replied, "My friend, do that for which you came." Then the soldiers seized and bound him.

There was great confusion, and Peter, in a rage, drew his sword and cut off the ear of one of the crowd. But the Master rebuked him, and said, "Put your sword up again, for all they that take the sword shall perish by the sword. Do you not think that I can not beseech my Father, and he shall even now send me more than twelve legions of angels? But how would the Scriptures be fulfilled?" Then he healed the wounded man and said to the crowd: "Have you come out with swords and clubs to seize me, as if I were a robber? I sat daily in the Temple teaching, but you did not take me. But this is your hour and the power of darkness, that the Scriptures of the prophets may be fulfilled."

Then all his disciples forsook him and fled; but Markos followed after to find out where they were going to take him, so that he could tell me; and, as they went, one of the crowd, seeing him, ran and seized hold of the sheet to arrest him, but Markos left the sheet in his hands and fled away naked and hid until he saw Lazarus. And so the despicable plot of the priests succeeded; yet only through the treachery of one of the Master's own followers, and by the Master's deliberate refusal to use his superhuman powers in his own defense.

One thing was particularly exasperating—the presence of our soldiers acting without any orders from me. In a rage I hurried through the cloisters into the Tower and found Petronius, my lieutenant, who was expecting me and had his answer ready.

"The priests came to me," he said, "with a warrant, signed and sealed by the procurator himself, ordering me to furnish a band of soldiers to apprehend Jesus of Nazareth and take him to the high priest. So I sent Longinus with some trusty fellows, and did not communicate with you because the order was addressed to me personally."

I was furious at this direct slighting of my authority by my superior, and was about hurrying off to hand in my resignation when I remembered the pallid face of Mary, who was anxiously waiting for news of where they had taken the Master. So it was not long before we were all at the entrance to the palace of Caiaphas, the high priest.

There I learned from some soldiers that the Master was being tried for blasphemy by the Sanhedrim, in their council-chamber, which adjoins the palace. I told one of them to take a message from me to Longinus, who was within, ordering him to see that Jesus was not harmed, and to remind Caiaphas that he had not the power of life and death.

As the soldier left, I was attracted by the sound of a violent altercation, and, near a fire which had been built in the court, I saw Simon Peter surrounded by a crowd of the high priest's servants, who were taunting him and saying that they knew he was one of the Nazarene's followers, as they had seen him with him, and, besides, he was a Galilean—his speech betrayed him. Peter became very violent, cursing and swearing, "I do not know this man of whom you speak." Just then a cock crew. The sound seemed to affect Peter strangely; he turned pale, trembled, and then, weeping, fled away.

And that is the way of the world. Even this most enthusiastic disciple, who had not feared to draw his sword in his Master's defense, now basely denied him and fled.

Mary saw this and turned to me trembling: "Will you desert him also, Caius?"

"No. I shall save him if I can. I am going to Pilate."

"I knew you would!" she exclaimed, with a look that made me feel truly blessed.

Just then John, who had also followed after the Master's captors, came out of the palace. I believe he is some connection of the high priest, and so had been admitted. Mary ran up and asked what had happened within.

"The Master has just declared that he is the Christ, the Son of the living God, and that they will see him sitting at the right hand of power, and coming with the clouds of heaven. The high priest has rent his clothes, declaring this to be rank blasphemy, and the Sanhedrim has declared the Master to be worthy of death."

With a low moan, Mary swooned into my arms. When we had with great difficulty revived her, I told her not to fear, as the Sanhedrim had no power to put the Master to death, and that I would hasten to Pilate to keep him from carrying out the sentence. I begged her to go home with Lazarus to break the dreadful news to the mother of Jesus and the other loving women there, and to assure them that I would leave nothing undone to save our beloved Master.

So she departed, and I hastened across the city to the Prætorium. It was now about sunrise. I found Pilate already dressed in his official robes, and with an anxious expression on his countenance. Before I could speak, he began to answer the question he knew well was on my lips:

"I know, dear Claudius, that you are justly irritated by my action in sending an order to your subordinate over your head; but just sit down and listen while I explain. It was the last thing I should think of doing—particularly as you are my favorite nephew—except in a case of great

318

emergency. You know these troublesome priests
have given me no peace in the matter of this mad
rabbi from Galilee, and they have been especially
annoying since you refused to interfere when he
drove out that pack of vulgar traders from the
Temple. You must realize that my position here
is none too secure. These Jews, as you know,
are hard enough to manage anyway, and they
have not had any love for me since that aqueduct
affair, when I had to rid the world of so many
rebellious rascals. And my superior, the proprætor Vitellius, I know does not hold me in any
particular affection, and also wants my place for
one of his own greedy family, so that he is ready
to do me an injury if he can get a chance. I
have been also informed that a deputation of
Samaritans has complained of me to him at
Antioch, on account of the bloody lesson I gave
them at Mount Gerizim last year, you remember.
And you know," he continued, lowering his voice,
"that our gracious and divine Cæsar is somewhat
inclined to suspicion, and enforces his favorite
law of *majestas*—really, you might say—with
some atrocity. So I feared that, if I should

have persisted in refusing to arrest a man who
has been so emphatically accused of sedition,
Vitellius or some other enemy might twist it into
a violation of the *leges majestatis*, and, if the
divine Cæsar took it up, then, my dear Claudius,
there would be nothing left for your uncle but
to take a warm bath and open his veins."

"But you know well that the Master is innocent
of any sedition."

"That is just why I have had him arrested
and have let them try him according to their
silly laws. They may condemn him——"

"They *have* condemned him—to death—for
blasphemy!"

"What is that to me? They can not execute
the penalty, and they will have to bring him to me
for final judgment, and I am convinced that he
is not guilty of any serious crime. That reply
of his about the tribute money—the one you told
me of—is evidence enough that he is not a poten-
tial rebel. So, when they bring him here, I shall
give him a fair trial and of course acquit him.
I did not send the warrant to you, because I knew
how much you think of the Nazarene, and, after

what he did for you, I can not blame you. Do you not see, my Claudius, that I have done the best thing possible under the circumstances?"

"Perhaps, but this I will say—you certainly did what you thought best for *us*."

"And I am sure that the outcome will prove that my action was well taken."

Just then we noticed a distant clamor, growing every moment louder. I looked out and saw coming up the narrow street a band of soldiers guarding the Master, whose hands were bound with cords. Behind them came a number of priests and councilors of the Sanhedrim, followed by a howling mob, who were hurling imprecations against the helpless prisoner.

As they came in front of the Prætorium I could see the Master plainly, and was amazed at his expression. It was one of perfect calm, the peace that passes all understanding. He stood there looking straight before him; but his eyes did not seem to see anything on earth—rather were they fixed upon an infinite distance, while an ineffable smile hovered about his lips. It was a marvelous contrast to the diabolical hatred that glowed

in the faces of the priests and to the wild fury of
the many-headed mob. It was not the smile of
contempt of a great soul like Anaxagoras, who,
when he was told that the Athenians had condemned him to die, replied, "And Nature, them";
it was something far higher. It gave me the feeling that the Master, if he saw fit, could sweep
that cowardly pack into annihilation with a word
—nay, even with a glance—and that his standing
there bound, a prisoner, was because he had so
willed it—willed to go through whatever might
befall. His was the look, not of a man, but of a
god.

A soldier entered with the request of the priests
who begged the procurator to come outside and
hear them, for their law would not permit them
to enter beneath a Gentile roof, as it would dis-
qualify them from taking part in the sacrifice of
the *Chagigah.*

"The sanctimonious villains!" muttered Pilate.
Then turning to the soldier, "Bring in the
prisoner, and tell those silly Jews that I grant
their request." Then, taking the insignia of his
office and beckoning me to follow, he went below.

BEFORE PILATE

As we passed through the court, I saw the Master standing by a pillar. I went up to him and said:
"I will do all I can for you."

There came into his unfathomable eyes a look of infinite sweetness.

"You shall have your reward, Caius Claudius," he said, "but you can do nothing. Only that can befall me which my Father wills—and his will be done!"

With a feeling of utter helplessness I followed Pilate out on the porch.

"What accusation do you bring against this man?" he asked the chief priest.

"If this fellow were not a malefactor we would not have delivered him to you."

"What do you think of that for an accusation, Caius?" said Pilate with a laugh. "But I shall answer them according to their own folly." And turning to the priests, "Then take him and judge him according to your own law."

"It is not lawful for us to put him to death; the case is one belonging to your jurisdiction," replied the high priest. "We found this fellow perverting the nation, and forbidding the people to give tribute to Cæsar, saying that he himself is Christ, a king."

"What liars they are!" remarked Pilate to me. "But you see the charge is grave enough for me to examine it." So he entered the court, and ordered the Master to be brought before him.

As the Master looked at him with that unfathomable gaze, I could see that Pilate was troubled. And, were it not for the bonds, one would think that the Master was the examiner, and the procurator the accused.

"Are you the King of the Jews?" Pilate managed to ask at last.

"Do you say this of yourself, or did others tell it to you about me?" the Master calmly asked in return. This irritated the procurator, and he burst forth:

"Am I a Jew? Your own people and the chief priests have delivered you to me. Now answer me; what are you?"

"My kingdom is not of this world; if my kingdom were of this world, then would my servants fight that I should not be delivered up to the Jews. But my kingdom is not from hence."

CHRIST BEFORE PILATE, from the painting by M. Munkacsy

"'What accusation do you bring against this man?'
he asked the chief priests. 'If this fellow was not a
malefactor we would not have delivered him to you.'"

BEFORE PILATE

"Are you a king, then?"

"You say it because I am a king. To this end was I born, and to this end have I come into this world, so that I should bear witness unto the truth. Every one that is of the truth hears my voice."

"What is truth?" asked Pilate with a light laugh, as he rose and went out on the porch.

Lucius, I have often asked that question and in the same tone; but that was before the Master healed me.

I also went out, and heard Pilate say, "I find no crime in him."

This was the occasion of a storm of accusations, several of the priests speaking at once, and the crowd murmuring and muttering. I could only make out: "He is stirring up the people everywhere, teaching his pernicious doctrines through all Judæa, beginning in Galilee, even to this place."

The word Galilee caught Pilate's ear.

"What did you say about Galilee?" he asked. "Is this man a Galilean?"

"Certainly. He comes from Nazareth in Galilee,"

"Then," said Pilate, with a sigh of relief, "he belongs to Herod's jurisdiction. I shall send the Nazarene to him." And, paying no attention to the objections of the high priests and the murmurs of the crowd, he turned on his heel and went within.

"Why, in Jove's name, did you do that, uncle?" I asked. "I fear Herod."

"Do not worry about him, Caius. He is too anxious to keep the favor of his wild Galileans to injure one they adore so much."

"But you remember John the Baptizer?"

"Certainly. But this Jesus has nothing to fear, unless he attacks Herod's beautiful wife; and he ought to have sense enough to take warning from John's fate. Then, you know, by thus recognizing Herod's jurisdiction, I think I shall conciliate him somewhat; and just now I need all the friends I can get."

"Let *me* take him to Herod."

"No—that would be beneath your dignity— Longinus can do that. But you may take my message to Herod, and—make it just as friendly as you can without impairing my dignity."

BEFORE PILATE

I thanked him and hurried away, not with any hopes of being able to aid the Master—for I felt as one in the meshes of inexorable fate—but from an overwhelming desire to see what he would do and say in the presence of this Oriental tyrant.

Herod was greatly pleased when I delivered the procurator's message, and said:

"You must give my thanks to Pontius Pilate for his consideration, and tell him that I thoroughly appreciate his courtesy, and will be always ready to oblige him in similar matters. Sit down here with me, Caius Claudius. We shall have him brought in here. I have long wanted to see some of his marvelous miracles."

Then he sent a message to Herodias and Salome, bidding them come and see the famous prophet and wonder-worker from Nazareth. In a few moments Salome appeared with the word that her mother was tired of prophets and wished to be excused. Herod laughed, and, bidding the little princess take her seat beside us, gave orders to admit the Nazarene and his accusers.

Salome flashed me a meaning glance—poor child!

UNDER PONTIUS PILATE

The Nazarene entered quietly and stood before us with that unfathomable look still in his eyes, while the priests violently repeated their accusation.

Herod then began to question him, but he did not answer a word. He looked into the distance, as if Herod and the raging throng of accusers did not exist. I looked at Herod and saw that he was totally nonplussed. What could this man mean?

"Prophesy unto me," he said. "I have long heard of your fame in Galilee as a great prophet. Tell me what is to be my fortune in the war."

But the Master remained silent. Herod bit his lip, and Salome leaned over and said with a sly glance at me:

"I think that this Nazarene is a great deal stupider than the Baptizer and a certain wise Roman I know of, for John and the Roman could talk, and talk well, too—tho they did not have much sense."

Then Herod rose and said:

"I have heard much of your wonderful powers, O prophet of Galilee. Show me one of your miracles, and I will set you free—nay, even protect you from your enemies. Come now, work me a miracle—one of your best."

But still the Master made no reply and his look did not change. Salome smiled and said:

"I am afraid we shall not have much of an entertainment to-day."

"If the Nazarene will not furnish one," said Herod with a hard laugh, "I shall have to undertake it myself. Listen, O Nazarene. It is said that you claim to be the King of the Jews, the Redeemer of Israel, of the royal line of David. You evidently do not deign to honor one who is but a son of the great Herod, the Idumean. So, then, I shall perforce be obliged to pay homage to you, O Son of David." He bowed low before the Master, with a scornful laugh, and ordered one of his servants to bring an old purple robe of his and throw it over the Nazarene's shoulders. Then addressing the guard, he said:

"Take back this mighty monarch to the Procurator, Pontius Pilate, for he is far beyond my puny power. Only Imperial Rome and the officers of the divine Cæsar are fit to cope with him.

Lead him thither in a state befitting his lofty dignity."

The soldiers quickly fell into Herod's humor, and, with ribald shouts and jests, escorted the prisoner out of the hall in a mock triumphal procession, followed by the priests, and joined outside by the mob.

Herod asked me to remain, but I hurried away, pleading business with the procurator, and reached the Prætorium some time before the procession, which was delayed, I imagine, by frequent stops to amuse the mob.

"Well, Caius," said Pilate as I entered, "Herod did not injure your Nazarene, did he?"

"No; but he sends him back to you."

"What for?"

"Jesus would not answer, and Herod could get nothing out of him."

"Oh!" sighed Pilate, wearily, "I shall have to finish this business myself. I wish I were well out of it." Then he ordered his judgment-seat to be placed on the porch, so that he might declare his decision with due formality.

The mob returned, following the Master and

his guard. It seemed as if the whole city were aroused. The clamor was so deafening and the disorder so threatening that the procurator ordered out his body-guard to keep the crowd at a respectful distance. But when he called the priests and the Sanhedrists together before his seat, a hush came over the multitude, who were straining their ears to hear the judgment.

"You have brought to me," Pilate said, "this man, as one who perverts the people. I have examined him and have found no fault in him concerning the things you accuse him of. Nor has Herod found any crime in him, for he has sent him back to me. And, truly, nothing worthy of death has been done by him. I will therefore chastise him and release him."

Some of the crowd having caught the last words cried out:

"It is the Passover. Release for us our prisoner."

It is the custom here, my Lucius, for the procurator, in honor of the great feast, to release whatever prisoner the people may choose.

"Very well," said Pilate, "I shall do so. Think now and decide whom I shall release."

UNDER PONTIUS PILATE

I could see, by the expression on my uncle's face, that he, like me, was sure that the vast multitude, which had escorted Jesus in triumph into the city and had hung upon his words for days, would choose *him* to be set free.

At this moment a servant came up to Pilate and said:

"Claudia Procula sends you word to have nothing to do with this righteous man. She says that she has suffered many things in a dream this day because of him." And then he lowered his voice so I could only catch disjointed phrases, evidently parts of the dream: "The Son of God— sitting on his throne in the heavens—judging all the world—we must not offend him."

Pilate turned pale and answered in a low tone: "Tell your mistress that I shall heed her admonition."

While this was going on I noticed that many of the priests and Sanhedrists had left the porch and were mingling with the crowd, passing rapidly from one to another. I could not imagine at first what they were doing, but I learned only too soon.

BEFORE PILATE

At length Pilate, rising and commanding silence, asked in a loud voice:

"What do you wish me to do? Shall I release unto you the King of the Jews?"

A roar came from the mob:

"Bar-Abbas! Bar-Abbas! Not this man, but Bar-Abbas!"

Now I saw what the priests had been about and what a child is this same many-headed mob. Pilate was completely dumfounded. That these people, who had so lately shouted hosannas to the "Son of David," should now cast him aside for a murderous robber, was beyond his understanding. Again he called out:

"What then shall I do with this Jesus, that is called the Christ?"

"Let him be crucified!" howled the mob, again and again. "Give us Bar-Abbas—and crucify Jesus!"

A chill struck through my heart. I looked within, where Jesus was. He stood in the same position, the same unfathomable look in his eyes.

"Why? What evil has he done?" shouted Pilate.

"Crucify him! crucify him!" yelled the mob.
Finding that he could not pacify them, the
procurator called for a basin of water and began
to wash his hands. The sight of this strange
action stilled the clamor for a space, and Pilate
spoke:

"I am innocent of the blood of this righteous
man. See you to it."

And the answer came howling back:

"His blood be upon us and upon our children!"
And the crowd swayed hither and thither, shout-
ing and screaming: "Crucify Jesus! Give us
Bar-Abbas!"

So great was the tumult that the guards were
even forced back a little space. And Pilate,
seeing that something had to be done to pacify the
mob, gave orders to the soldiers within to scourge
Jesus.

Then the crowd quieted down, listening to the
whistling blows of the scourge, and hoping also
to hear the usual screams. But no such sounds
came from the Prætorium. I could not force
myself to look within while the torture was going
on, nor afterward, when I heard the soldiers—

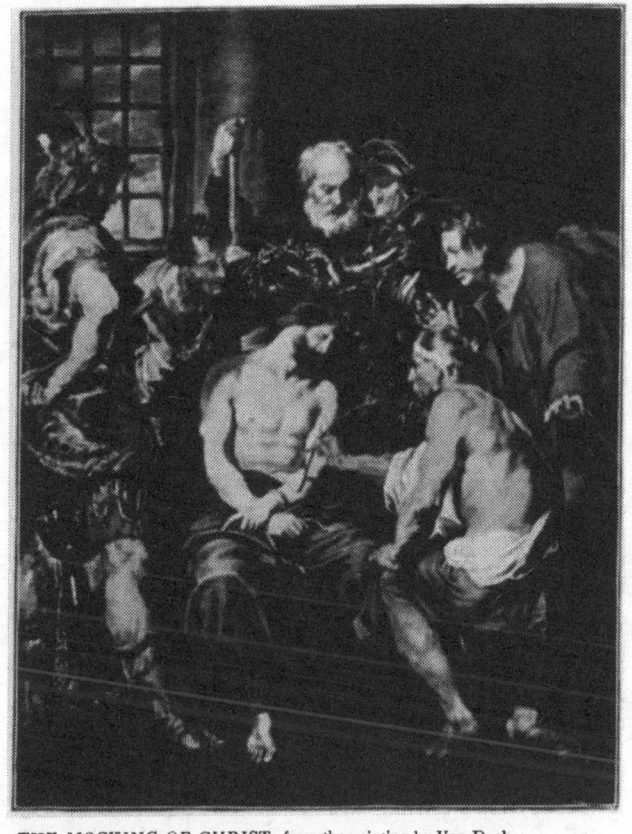

THE MOCKING OF CHRIST, from the painting by Van Dyck

"The soldiers . . . mocking their victim with coarse jests and calling out in derision, 'Hail! King of the Jews!'"

as is their wont—mocking their victim with coarse jests and calling out in derision, "Hail! King of the Jews!"

Finally the procurator, seeing the mob was again getting uneasy, went within and returned, leading the Master, who had on him Herod's old purple robe and a crown of thorns that some soldier had plaited and placed upon his head. I can not conceive what Pilate meant by this. Perhaps he may have thought that the sight of the innocent victim after so much suffering would turn their hearts to pity. Placing Jesus beside the judgment-seat, he said, in compassionate accents:

"Behold the man!"

But the priests and their followers called out:

"Crucify him! crucify him!" And the empty-headed mob repeated the cry.

"Then take him yourselves and crucify him," cried Pilate, impatiently, "for I find no crime in him."

"We have a law," the high priest said, " and by that law he ought to die, because he made himself the Son of God."

Pilate turned pale. "The Son of God!—Claudia's dream!" he murmured.

Then he took the Master once more within. I followed.

"Whence are you?" asked Pilate anxiously.

But Jesus gave him no answer.

"Why do you not speak to me?" he asked again. "Do you not know that I have power to release you, and power to crucify you?"

Then the Master answered:

"You would have no power against me unless it were given you from above. Therefore he that delivered me unto you has the greater sin."

"I shall do what I can for you," said the procurator. And once more he went out and spoke to the people.

"Do you not wish that I release this Jesus also? He has committed no crime worthy of death, and surely he has suffered enough for what he may have done. I am willing to release him also."

But the high priest called out in a sinister tone:

"If you release this man, you are not Cæsar's friend. Every one that makes himself a king opposes Cæsar."

336

And the crowd took up the cry, "You are not Cæsar's friend."

The shot went home. Pilate trembled and turned pale. The coward in him was now uppermost. I could see that he was thinking of Vitellius's hate and the divine Cæsar's suspicion; for it was in a tone of great bitterness that he said once more:

"Behold your king!"

"Away with him! away with him!" yelled the mob. "Crucify him!"

"Shall I crucify your king?"

"We have no king but Cæsar," answered the high priest. And the mob took up the cry, "We have no king but Cæsar."

Then Pilate, with a hopeless look, took his place on the judgment-seat and said:

"Let Bar-Abbas be released; and let Dysmas and Gestas, robbers, and Jesus of Nazareth, the King of the Jews, be crucified."

Everything whirled about me. The cries of the multitude sounded like the rushing of many winds. But when I gathered my senses together and looked at the Master, he stood there calm and unmoved, and the light of heaven shone in his eyes.

Then I heard Pilate's voice, coming as from an infinite distance:

"Longinus, you will take charge of the crucifixion; and you, Caius Claudius, will return to the citadel and put the garrison under arms. But do not sally forth without express orders from me, unless you see actual fighting. We can take no risks to-day."

And here I am—writing to keep myself from going mad. The garrison is under arms, watching on the battlements. On a little hill just outside the walls, three crosses are standing—bearing their writhing burdens. Beneath them I can see Longinus with the guard, and a little group of women. It is past the ninth hour—the darkness has passed away, and the earth has ceased to tremble—the sun is slowly sinking in the west— it seems as if the world must come to an end— for, Lucius,—Jesus, the Master, was the Son of God.

GOLGOTHA, from the painting by Jean-Léon Gérome

"On a little hill just outside the walls, three crosses are standing."

XXIII

The Tomb

XXIII

At Jerusalem

IT is the evening of the Sabbath. I am calmer than I was yesterday, my Lucius, tho on my soul is a heavy load which will not lift. The Master had become so much to me—had so entered into my life—that it seems as tho I could not exist since he is gone. Yet I live on, and so do the others who loved him. But how?

Yesterday evening, about the tenth hour, Syrus came in, pale and trembling—he could scarcely stand. I had wine brought, which somewhat revived him; and then, in disjointed fashion, he told me this tale:

"Master, I followed the procession to Golgotha —I saw Jesus fall under the cross—I saw them place it on another—I saw him nailed upon it and raised between the two thieves—I heard him say, 'Father, forgive them, for they know not what they do.'—I heard the jeers and the taunts of the priests and of the multitude, and even of Gestas who hung beside him—I heard Dysmas ask him to remember him when he came into his kingdom—I heard the Master promise him that he should be that day with him in Paradise.— And he looked like a god, hanging there upon the cross.—And when the darkness came upon us I fell upon my face and was afraid—and what happened for a time, I know not.—At last I heard Jesus cry with a loud voice, 'My God, my God, why hast thou forsaken me?' I rose and listened—and he said, 'Father, into thy hands I commend my spirit'—and after a space, 'It is finished.'—Then all was still—except that Longinus cried out in terror, 'Of a truth, this is the Son of God!'

"But when the earth began to quake and rock, I fled into the vale of Hinnom—there I met Judas —Judas, the traitor—and his face was the face of a lost soul.—When he saw me he cried, 'Away from me! I have betrayed innocent blood,' and fled swiftly up the hill.—I sank down from fear and exhaustion.—A little while after, the earth ceased to tremble—the sun burst through the clouds—and I saw above me a man hanging from the branch of a tree over the abyss—a rope was about his neck—and he swung back and forth horribly.—Then the branch broke, and he crashed down right at my feet and burst asunder on the sharp rocks.—It was Judas—his dead face was the face of a demon—and once more I fled away.

"Protect me, master, for I am full of sin.—In truth Jesus was the Christ—the Son of God—and we—fools and blind—rejected him and his kingdom—because it was not of this world, but was of heaven and love and the spirit of God. And now I see it all—too late—too late! Help me, master."

I tried to console him, and in the effort grew myself more calm. But his misery is boundless and his despair beyond consolation.

To-day I went to the home of Lazarus, where the faithful women and some of the disciples are gathered. I found them in the court, bowed down with an immeasurable sorrow, utterly without hope. The mother of the Master sat in their midst. She was not weeping, but her noble face showed a wo the like of which I have never seen. John sat beside her and held her hand—Mary told me that the Master on the cross entrusted his mother to John's care. On the other side sat Peter, in abject despair because he had denied his Master and had not died with him.

I offered them my protection, in case the chief priests should extend their persecution to the followers of the Master; but, tho they thanked me, I could see that it made no difference to them whether they lived or followed their beloved Master into the shades of death. And in truth, my Lucius, for my part I do not feel that my own life is worth living now that he is gone.

I did not remain long, and, as I took my leave, Mary went with me to the door. There she told me briefly that Nicodemus and Joseph had begged the body of Jesus from Pilate, and just at sundown had hastily buried it in a new tomb. She, with the other women who had come from Galilee, had seen where they had laid him, and had prepared spices and myrrh, and to-morrow in the

early morning they would go and embalm him
as was fitting.

"But what will you do then, Mary?" I asked.

"I do not know. But, Caius, in spite of all,
there is something within me that keeps on saying
that it is *not* ended. He said once that he would
go away, and would come again."

"How can he come again—now that he is
dead and buried?"

"I do not know. Yet he raised Larazus——"

"But then *he* was alive—and now he is gone
from us forever."

"So Peter says, and so says John. I may be
foolish, but I feel still within me that he will come
again. How—I know not—but in his own good
time—in his own good way—for he could not say
what was untrue.—And now, may God bless and
keep you, Caius! You have been so good to us
all." And, taking my hand, she kissed me upon
the forehead. I feel that the benediction of that
holy kiss is with me yet.

Pilate has granted a guard, to watch over the
tomb, for the chief priests fear that the Master's
disciples may steal his body away, and give out

that he has risen from the dead.   As if the poor
heart-broken band could attempt anything!—
Yet, if the Master *should* arise from the dead
he would indeed be God.

But that is impossible.

XXIV

The Risen Lord

XXIV

At Jerusalem

LUCIUS, I fear that you will not believe what I write to you; nor can I blame you if you do not, for it transcends all human understanding. But yet it is true.

The Master has risen from the dead! He is alive—among us—and he is the Lord our God! How can I tell it to you?

This morning I went with Syrus and Longinus —who also believes—to assist the women in rolling away the stone from before the tomb. But the tomb was empty and the guard gone.

As I turned away, I saw Mary sitting under a tree near by, her face radiant as if it were the face of an angel. The moment she saw me she came running and exclaiming:

"Caius, Caius, rejoice! rejoice! the Master

349

has risen—I have seen him and touched him!"
And she flung herself upon my neck, weeping
for very joy.

"But, Mary," said I, when she became a little
calm, "you do not mean that Jesus is alive again?"
For I could by no means bring myself to believe
what she said.

"Let me tell you the whole story, Caius, and
then you will not doubt. This morning early,
before it was yet light, we three women started
for the tomb; but I ran ahead of the others and
got there first. The stone was rolled away—the
tomb was empty. And tho the Master had told
us that he would come again—my poor, distracted mind could not believe it *then*—I know
not why—but I thought the priests had taken him
away.

"So I ran back, and found John and Peter,
and cried, 'They have taken away the Master
out of the tomb, and I know not where they have
laid him.' Then they two started running,
and I after them—but I could not keep up, and
when I reached the tomb again, they had gone;
and for a time I stood outside and wept. After

a while I looked within and saw two bright ones sitting there, and they asked, 'Woman, why do you weep?' And I replied, 'Because they have taken away the Master, and I know not where they have laid him.'

"Then I saw them no more. But when, after a time, I turned to go back—my eyes blinded with tears—I was aware of some one standing near, who also asked, 'Woman, why do you weep? Whom do you seek?' I thought it must be the gardener, and said, 'Sir, if you have borne him hence, tell me where you have laid him and I will take him away.' Then I heard the dear voice say, 'Mary,'—and I knew it was he, and crying 'Master!' I flung myself down before him and clasped his feet. But he, withdrawing himself a little, said in his old, loving tone: 'Take not hold on me, for I am not yet ascended unto the Father. But go to my brethren, and say to them, 'I ascend unto my Father and your Father and my God and your God.' And then I saw him no more."

I returned with Mary to the house of Lazarus. There was Mary, the mother of John, and Salome.

UNDER PONTIUS PILATE

They too had seen the Master and had worshiped him. And he had charged them to tell the disciples to go back into Galilee, for there they should behold him.

And now, my beloved Lucius, you may never see me again. I too believe in the Lord Jesus Christ, the Son of God the Father. My old life is dead and the new life begins. I can not, in any way that you could understand, explain how it has come about. But it is so. I understand now what the Master said to us. I know I have the Truth, and the Truth has made me free. The Truth and Love; for all bitterness and hatred have passed from my soul, and I love and cherish all men, my brethren, even those who crucified the Master, and who may perhaps persecute us, his disciples.

But, with them, I am willing to undergo whatever our Father may send us; for what does this short span of life count with us who have eternity for our inheritance—eternity with our loving Father and his beloved Son? I am no longer a Roman, a Claudius, I am merely a man— one of the sons of our Father who is in heaven.

THE RISEN LORD

I have given up my office, and, with Syrus and Susanna and Longinus, I shall follow Mary and the brethren into Galilee to meet our risen Lord.— Farewell.